The Rise and Fall
of
Kwame Nkrumah

The Rise and Fall
of
Kwame Nkrumah

A Study of Personal Rule in Africa

HENRY L. BRETTON

FREDERICK A. PRAEGER, *Publishers*

New York • Washington • London

FREDERICK A. PRAEGER, *Publishers*
111 Fourth Avenue, New York, N.Y. 10003, U.S.A.
77–79 Charlotte Street, London W.1, England

Published in the United States of America in 1966
by Frederick A. Praeger, Inc., Publishers

©1966 by Frederick A. Praeger, Inc.
Library of Congress Catalog Card Number: 66–26548

Printed in the United States of America

To
Marian, Elizabeth, and Alexander

Preface

The idea of writing a book on personal rule in Africa suggested itself to me nearly ten years ago when I first came into contact with Kwame Nkrumah and observed his political style. At that time, I saw absolutely no signs of democratic orientation in him or in any of his close collaborators. These people wanted power and were acquiring it as rapidly as possible. All one could really say for Nkrumah and his regime was that he deserved the benefit of the doubt in view of the situation he had inherited.[1]

As the years passed, the thought of analyzing the Nkrumah variant of the age-old pattern of personal rule leading to undisputed leadership and finally to despotism interested me increasingly.

An invitation by the University of Ghana to assist in the development of its political-science program provided the opportunity for an extended sojourn. While I meticulously avoided involvement in Ghanaian affairs, I felt free to pursue my research interests. These were materially furthered by a state of underemployment, a consequence of Presidential pressure and intervention in university affairs. One overcautious Ghanaian colleague, apprehensive of possible Presidential displeasure with my non-Nkrumaist lectures, even suggested that I leave lecturing to others and pursue instead studies of "some tribe upcountry." When Nkrumah, in the course of an interview, admonished me to be "intellectually honest" in my writings about Ghana, I decided then and there to oblige by writing a book addressed to the core problem of Ghana—namely, Kwame Nkrumah and his political machine.

Materials for this book were gathered over a ten-year period, in particular during visits to Ghana in 1956, 1959, 1962, and during my extended stay in 1964–65.

I gratefully acknowledge the assistance rendered by the Rockefeller Foundation, whose grant to the University of Michigan enabled me to serve one year at the University of Ghana at

Legon and the following year at the University College Nairobi, Kenya. The University of Michigan assisted directly by supplementing the grant out of its Developing Areas Fund and by administering the entire grant. My colleagues in the Department of Political Science at Michigan contributed by agreeing to let me serve in Africa for two years. My thanks go also to the University of Ghana, Legon, and its faculty and staff for trying to make us comfortable under most difficult circumstances. I am greatly indebted to the University College Nairobi and to Dr. Arthur T. Porter, its Principal, for it was largely during my stay there that the book was written.

At Legon, circumstances somewhat restricted the circle of friends and the opportunities for political discourse. Nothing, however, could suppress or restrain the wit, perspicacity, and cordial professional fellowship of Dr. Conor Cruise O'Brien, then the Vice Chancellor of the university. He and his wife, Maire, were constant sources of succor and inspiration. My wife and children shared with me the benefits of their presence at Legon. Among my Ghanaian colleagues, most of whom were under a cloud of political distrust and suspicion, very few braved the Nkrumaist injunction against socializing with foreigners. We were doubly appreciative, therefore, of the friendship and hospitality extended to us by those who dared.

Martin Kilson's penetrating observations and Richard Esseks' accounts of his experiences were of great value, and I thank them. Several of my expatriate colleagues at Legon, although unwittingly, allowed me to test my ideas on them: the foremost being Tony Killick, whose advice on certain aspects of the economic situation was invaluable, Preston King, and Jitandra Mohan.

Because of the position he occupied at the time, I particularly appreciated the courteous treatment accorded to me by Kofi Baako in the one extended discussion that circumstances permitted us to have. The same applies to W. M. Q. Halm.

The late Dr. J. B. Danquah, whom I had the privilege of interviewing on two occasions before his final incarceration and death in prison, provided glimpses of Nkrumah's personality that only he could have seen. In the same political camp, I was privileged to talk, over the years, to Peggy and Joe Appiah. Not only were both most valuable sources of information, but their quiet heroism, especially during Joe's detention, served as a constant spur to me to produce this book.

David M. Williams, editor of *West Africa,* was most helpful with suggestions drawn from his vast store of knowledge on West African affairs. The assistance of J. H. Mensah, K. B. Ayensu, and M. A. Bentil was greatly appreciated. I also wish to extend my appreciation to Daniel Chapman for his assistance when I first came to Ghana and for his reactions to my comments on subsequent occasions. His pointers proved to be invaluable. To Professor and Mrs. William B. Harvey, my appreciation for sharing with me some of their experiences in Ghana and for their practical advice and assistance.

To the numerous other contacts and personal friends, in Ghana and elsewhere, who provided information, answered my questions, and were of assistance in other respects, I extend my sincere thanks.

I wish to record here my deep appreciation for the willingness of my wife, Marian, to accept my many months of absence from home, for her willingness to brave the hazards of life under Nkrumah, and for her cool and detached judgment in delicate situations. She also critically evaluated certain portions of the book and assisted with the typing.

None of the above-mentioned persons, institutions, and agencies—with the sole exception of the author, of course—should be held responsible for the contents of this book, for the inevitable errors and omissions, or for its conclusions.

Mrs. E. M. McArthur's secretarial assistance in typing most of the manuscript was, of course, indispensable.

H. L. B.

Nairobi
June 25, 1966

Contents

The Rise and Fall
of
Kwame Nkrumah

Introduction

In my previous work on government and politics in Africa, I have endeavored to maintain a sense of realism.[1] I have always entertained doubts concerning the validity and relevance of many generalizations and of certain concepts developed in literature about political behavior and political institutions. My extended sojourn on the continent from 1964 to 1966, in both West and East Africa, has reinforced my doubts.

One should not take for granted that political processes and political behavior are governed by an orderly, mechanical, cause-and-effect relationship. Neither should one allow oneself to become hypnotized by concepts like "political parties," "administration," even "government," to the point where one fails to consider alternate ways of viewing things. Reading contemporary accounts of politics in developing areas, one gains, despite passing references to political change, the impression that the political scene is relatively fixed, endowed with ascertainable boundaries, and that the component parts of the developing polity are even capable of "behaving" so that the behavioral patterns can be projected and predicted. It may be more appropriate and useful to view the political scene in developing areas (perhaps everywhere) as an unfolding, multidimensional, kaleidoscopic panorama that reverses itself occasionally. Thus order, regularity, and uniformity may be statistically perceptible only over a long period of time and on the basis of a far larger body of evidence than is available at this juncture.[2]

Many of the sweeping generalizations found in contemporary scholarship concerning "one-party systems," "political modernization," "ideology," the "mass party," and "nation-building" treat legendary, ephemeral, certainly only peripheral aspects of political life in Africa. Some social-science specialists in the politics of development have fallen victim to recent developments not only in the politics of the countries studied but also

3

in the social sciences themselves. Caught up in the dual trends toward general systems analysis of social and political phenomena and at the same time a more immediate concern with man and his behavior, too many social scientists have succumbed to making ever more sweeping generalizations. They have steadily broadened their analytical frameworks to advance more impressive theoretical propositions that, alas, usually rest on exceedingly slight empirical evidence. Described regularities upon close analysis may prove to be wholly illusory. A generalization may seem real only because the evidence presented is itself an untested generalization: Scholar X seeks to prove the validity of his generalization by reference to Scholar Y. Wide gaps in the cause-and-effect relationships essential to validation of a generalization are simply ignored or "bridged" by mere terminological innovations.

The confluence of new conceptual and methodological concerns in the social sciences with the emergence of a large number of independent states in Africa has resulted in underdeveloped analytic techniques being applied to these new countries, so that much of the contemporary scholarship on the developing areas is highly speculative, hypothetical, and unrealistic.[3] Also, partly because of a traditional disinclination to probe deeply into social phenomena—for fear of adverse community reaction—and partly because of the sensitivity manifested by the newly independent regimes, scholarship has shown a preference for "antiseptic" analyses of politics. Mismanagement, corruption, in fact, the subject of money itself, are omitted from discussions of governmental systems;[4] examples of inconsistency, irrationality and caprice are ignored or undervalued; and any economic or social malfunction of systems is given short shrift. Everything develops; nothing decays.

Before we can offer the world valid generalizations concerning "value allocation," "socialization," and "modernization," more close-contact, country-by-country analyses have to be undertaken. Many more variables, alleged to be known but actually unknown, have to be identified, assessed, and interpreted. More has to be discovered about the nature and function of social change. Most crucial to an increase in substantive knowledge concerning political behavior is a heightened concern with man, with the real actors in politics and the real motivational forces. Much of social-science scholarship is cluttered with false leads; value is attached to what is merely prominent, to formal structural references.

Thus, besides attempting a conceptual reorientation and a review of some current generalizations, this study is intended to turn our attention to the center of the political scene. Applying systems and political behavior analysis where appropriate and borrowing from all disciplines within the social sciences, I have attempted a political analysis of core factors.

Specifically, the study examines the operational aspects of government, as distinct from the formal, assertive aspects. The possibility that government is being conducted on a personal, *ad hoc* basis in a highly irregular, possibly unpredictable fashion is examined. The nature and role of the sole political party is assessed, employing theoretical concepts less rigidly wedded to concern with parties and allowing for the possibility that the "party" is a euphemism for something else. The nature and role of what generally is termed "ideology" is closely examined in the light of communication theory with a view to reassessing its social function as well as some assumptions underlying current thought on the subject. Above all, the study is concerned with the role and function of one political personality—Kwame Nkrumah.

Given the diminutive size of the politically relevant population in Ghana, the state of communications, the economic and physical control structure and other politically restrictive aspects, it seems to me that the emphasis in most literature dealing with modern Ghana—on broad social movement, political parties, and legal, social, and political institutions—is misplaced. Nkrumah and his political machine, controlling the key points in state and society, must be the focal point of a political assessment of Ghana between 1957 and 1966, and possibly for the period from 1951 to 1957 as well.

In one form or another, political machines have existed everywhere throughout history. West and East alike have known them and have suffered from them. In recent times, political machines have been in particular evidence in Latin America and Asia. A growing number of other newly independent states in Africa are controlled by them.

The use of the term "machine" should not suggest any resemblance to conventional mechanical devices since it does not obey the laws of physics or mechanics. It appears to function reliably only for one purpose: It was instrumental in Nkrumah's seizure of power and it kept him at the pinnacle for nearly a decade. For broader social purposes, however, it proved to be a most unreliable instrument. In that broader context, it might be viewed more appropriately as a time-space machine capable of moving both forward and backward, but not responsive in a conventional, predictable fashion to stimuli, or "inputs," to use a concept much in vogue these days. It has built-in delayed-action response, is unpredictable, behaves in an erratic manner, and tends to consume itself. Most important, it is a device controlled, to the extent that it is susceptible to control, by one man who, although he knows its general outline, is unequipped to understand all its propensities and all the likely consequences of its manipulation and use. It is a device very much like the magic broom brought to life by the overeager but unsophisticated "Sorcerer's Apprentice."

Maurice Duverger, French student of political organisms, describes the political machine as "an unofficial organization in the hands of the bosses and their followers."[5] It is in that sense that the term is used in the present study. Constructed by the supreme "boss," Nkrumah, the Ghanaian machine was built into and around the official organization of government and administration. At first, it hollowed out the existing structure; then it proceeded to crush the remaining shell. It represented the real, as against the formal, core of power and politics in Nkrumaist Ghana. Thus, Nkrumah's famous dictum "Seek ye first the political kingdom and all other things will be added unto you" could be interpreted as referring to the early establishment and maintenance of a personal political machine.

A few final observations concerning the critical tenor of this book: After I published *Power and Stability in Nigeria,* in 1962, a colleague commented that it was very good, "but how about getting back into the country?" Actually, not only did the political leaders of Nigeria welcome the criticism implied in that book, but a number of them wanted more of it. It seems to me that there is something wrong with the indulgent attitude taken by many observers of the contemporary political scene in Africa.

Sometime in the early stages of the African revolution—with whose broad social and humanitarian objectives I fully identify myself now, as I did then—Western intellectuals slipped into a state of mind that I can only describe as myopic sentimentality. Perhaps a collective feeling of guilt helped produce this euphoric willingness to disregard certain facts.

The greatest disservice that writers and scholars can do to the people of Africa is to treat their emerging political institutions and practices indulgently. Since nothing is likely to occur on the African continent that has not been experienced in one form or another on all other continents, one should extend all the benefits of scholarly analysis to events in Africa, letting the chips fall where they may. To treat emergent Africa as though it were in a state of intellectual quarantine, where criticism is to be postponed and only praise dare be given, is to consign the millions of that much tormented continent to further misery.

I

Background to Personal Rule

Traditionally, background studies on contemporary African affairs commence with a chronologically arranged summary of selected historical references. Certain events are said to have caused certain developments simply because the former preceded the latter in time and within certain geographic limits. There is the usual bow in the direction of Africa's mythical, uncharted past, the given country's ecology, traditional institutions and practices, village "democracy," and vague allusions to the "African Personality." In general, I am skeptical about methods of analysis, often no more than historiographic sleights of hand, which seek to link conclusively broad social movements or events to political institutions or behavior patterns. Restricting the analysis to the top-level control of the power and influence structure and leaving aside political ritual and ceremonial, I find assertions of historical progression and causal relationships linking Nkrumah's political machine to Africa's, or Ghana's, past quite unconvincing. I entertain similar doubts about the conduct of politics elsewhere in Africa.

The personal political machine has not evolved in a straight linear pattern within Ghana, West Africa, or even the African continent. It has developed in a highly irregular, sometimes irrational, and unsystematic fashion, and it has been rooted in a great variety of culturally and politically unrelated geographic areas. If progression it is, it defies systematic methods of historical analysis.

Identification of the dominant political style or culture in Nkrumaist Ghana as "non-Western" would be quite misleading. The roots of Nkrumah's political machine may be found in the United States, Great Britain, and the Soviet Union; in small circles of revolutionary enthusiasts and conspirators in London, Paris, and New York. They may be found in the writings of Jefferson, Lincoln, Marx, Lenin, Mazzini, Marcus Garvey, W. E. B. DuBois, and George Padmore; in the experiences of the British Labour Party, the Communist International, and various Fascist parties. Because the era of African awakening has been characterized by sharp, incisive social change and unprecedented technological innovations, and because the political leaders of Nkrumaist Ghana were, by and large, young, inexperienced and only too human—hence, prone to be diverted by opportunity—they, and particularly Kwame Nkrumah, were very much at sea in ever more bewildering and perplexing surroundings. Given to simplistic generalization, they moved much of the time in a make-believe world.

With the return of Kwame Nkrumah to the Gold Coast in 1947, after more than ten years of study and work abroad, a rudimentary political policy, conceived in London, New York, and Paris was introduced to an unsuspecting, generally disinterested country, the bulk of whose population was completely unequipped to comprehend its true nature, let alone to put up any resistance to it.[1] Tactics and practices were imported that bore no relationship to either the culture or polity in Ghana. For example, Nkrumah's creation, the Convention People's Party, was in its organization as well as its ideology closely patterned after the Communist parties in the Soviet Union and Eastern Europe. If the new tactics and political practices *appeared* to be related to Ghana's past, this was an illusion created by the academic habit of forcing events into a neat, consistent, and if possible, symmetrical historical mold, and by the incessant invocation of nationalist cant.[2]

If the personal political machine must be related to Ghana's past, even the recent past, this should be done not with a view to discovering linear antecedents but with the more modest objective of merely noting that certain conditions may have played a contributory role in its evolution. In that vein and without suggesting that the list is definitive or exhaustive, one might consider the following conditions: the cultural and psychological void arising from the colonial experience; the emphatically authoritarian bent of the colonial regime; and the social and economic retardation in Ghana at the time of independence.

THE CULTURAL, PSYCHOLOGICAL, AND POLITICAL VOID

I had occasion to interview the President of Ghana, Dr. Kwame Nkrumah, on January 15, 1965. At that time, he stressed, in rebuttal to critical assessment of his rule, that the colonial regime had left Ghana in a most deplorable state, and he made reference to the generally underdeveloped state of Ghana's economy, educational system, and cultural and social fabric. What Nkrumah may well have been aware of but was not prepared to admit was that the colonial experience had left Ghana a cultural wasteland fertile for little else but his political machine.

To be sure, Ghana possessed a cultural heritage and social and political traditions. However, very little of that heritage was of practical relevance or of functional value in the solution of Ghana's pressing social and economic-development problems. What was more important was that very little, if anything, in Ghana's past was of functional value in the construction of a modern political machine. Traditional social institutions and practices had value only in political ritual, and there only to a limited extent.[3] The colonial regime, in accordance with its central purpose, had blocked the development of a spirit of citizenship, a sense of modern social community development, and an aesthetic orientation meaningful to a people seeking contact with the mid-twentieth century.

Colonialism had no appreciable interest in the intellect or

the soul. (I am ignoring the concerns of the religious missions.) Crass materialism, cultural vacuity, and social vulgarity, cynicism and unbridled pragmatism, all seasoned with racialism—the black races being treated as genetically unfit for self-rule—could only evoke a crassly materialistic, politically crude, and cynical African response.

One aspect of the cultural void was the absence of relevant and socially and psychologically meaningful national symbols. This situation was ready-made, first, for the introduction of the personality of Nkrumah as a central rallying and unifying force, and then, for the development of the personality cult. From the beginning, Nkrumah and his principal radical supporters realized that strict personal rule would better enable them to survive the political setbacks to be expected in a weak and inexperienced country. In December, 1965, an editorial in the ideological organ of the party, *The Spark*, explained:

> The charismatic personality of President Nkrumah is one of the props on which the new nation of Ghana is built. It is not mere personality worship. It is the most practical way of providing the new ship of state with a stable keel. If a young nation cannot anchor itself down to a few basic concepts and rules of practice, there is an air of drifting which is most injurious to national evolution. And these principles must be crystallised in a person with whom, as a result of his personal efforts and sacrifices, the broad masses associate their yearnings for a better life.

Certainly, the cultural void and absence of socially meaningful national symbols contributed to the increasing reliance on the symbolic value provided by Nkrumah's striking personality and public posture. And the rejection by his more fervent supporters of the psychological props derived from religious beliefs most likely served as a further stimulant to the creation of the personality cult.

THE AUTHORITARIAN COMMITMENT

The colonial regime, beneath a thin veneer of democratic formalism, rested essentially on a highly centralized, hierarchical, authoritarian administration that was deliberately somewhat militaristic. As a matter of policy, the democratic content of the political system at home was not passed on to the subject peoples.[4] It appears that a more or less determined effort was made, behind a smokescreen of constitutionality, to extend to the African successor regime not the heritage of the Westminster model of parliamentary democracy but the authoritarian features of the colonial administration.[5]

Sometime in 1949, possibly a little earlier—in response to the widespread 1948 riots in what was then the Gold Coast, in the wake of the economic disaster of World War II, and in response to other pressures against British colonial policy elsewhere in the world—a decision was made in London to accelerate the Gold Coast's progress toward self-government and political independence. A prime consideration underlying that decision was the fact that the little colony then represented one of the Empire's major sources of dollar earnings.[6]

Although regarded initially as a wholly undesirable partner, by 1951 Nkrumah became the chosen instrument of the colonial regime to guide his country through what was envisaged as a peaceful transition period; though political power would be transferred, the country would remain within a web of British financial, commercial, and military interests. First as Leader of Government Business—a post to which he was appointed straight out of prison—then as Prime Minister, Nkrumah was loyally and effectively guided and supported by the Colonial Governor, Sir Charles Arden-Clarke. The Governor, no doubt reluctantly, appears to have done little against and a great deal for the eventual introduction of what Nkrumah in his autobiography calls "emergency measures of a totalitarian kind."[7]

To cite just a few illustrations of the relationship: In the course of the 1956 general election, which was represented to the public as a quasi referendum on the proposed constitution under which the colony was to attain political independence, it became apparent to the colonial authorities that violations of the election code had been so widespread as to raise doubts about the validity of the over-all election results—i.e., the overwhelming victory of Nkrumah's Convention People's Party (CPP). But the Governor opted in favor of overlooking the substantial body of evidence indicating a nearly total breakdown of the election machinery in some constituencies. Not a single constituency election result was set aside. Even Prime Minister Nkrumah himself had publicly defied a provision of the electoral code that prohibited invocation of tribal gods for electioneering purposes. A photograph placing him at the locale of the violation was published on the front page of a British-controlled daily paper, but was ignored by the colonial regime, which a few years earlier would have imprisoned him for a lesser infraction. An editor of the daily told me that toward the end of the campaign political murders had been so numerous that the British Government would have been compelled to cancel the election if the total had been published. They were not published.

Accordingly, when Ghana became independent, on March 6, 1957, it was in part on the basis of constitutional arrangements amicably negotiated between the incoming Ghanaian regime and the colonial power. But the political reality did not favor a constitutional system of government. Neither the departing colonial power, including the now Governor-General, Sir Arden-Clarke, nor the Ghanaian successor regime, was interested in upholding the constitutional order beyond paying it mere lip service and judicial skirmishing.[8] By all indications, the 1956 constitution, like so many other independence constitutions in Africa, failed from the moment of its inception to be an effective barrier to imposition of extraconstitutional personal rule.

It was to be less than one year before Nkrumah proceeded in earnest to dismantle the so-called constitutional system.[9]

SOCIAL AND ECONOMIC RETARDATION AND LACK OF CONTROL

On the economic balance sheet, Nkrumah inherited a country relatively well endowed with manpower and material resources. Compared with other emergent African and Asian states, Ghana, at independence, had one of the highest per-capita rates of capital reserve, one of the highest per-capita rates of income—just over £50—and one of the highest per-capita rates of trained middle- and lower-level public-service personnel.[10] However these assets were more than counterbalanced by the staggering needs of the young country—and by the fact that the departing colonial regime had barely prepared the new country to meet these needs. The relatively large number of trained civil servants was impressive only if viewed against the modest requirements of the colonial administration. Moreover, the training was geared largely to the requirements of expatriate commercial interests. The country was dependent upon what was essentially a one-crop economy. As late as 1965, 66 per cent of total export earnings were derived from the sale of cocoa. This situation was exacerbated by the sharp, unpredictable price fluctuations on the international commodity market.[11] Measured against generally accepted minimum standards of living, critical development gaps existed in such vital sectors as health and education, power production for even modest production goals, communication and transportation. Furthermore, sharp differences in levels of development separated the Northern Territories of Ghana from the more highly favored coastal region.

On balance, Ghana was, and is, poor, and the governmental, administrative, and political problems flowing from the relative poverty of the country were compounded by other drains on scarce resources: by hasty, often indiscriminate Africanization; by the decision to adopt from Communist countries obsolete and socially and economically irrelevant ideological formulas; by overextension of international commitments; through frivolous expenditures by a prestige-conscious regime; and by the corruption that inevitably saps the energies and scarce resources of young, inexperienced countries.[12]

The resultant pressures would have constituted a severe challenge to even a modest program of economic and social development. In the face of Nkrumah's ambitious goals for Ghana and for the African continent as a whole, political short cuts suggested themselves as possible answers to the mounting problems.

One major spur to the rapid Africanization of political and administrative agencies and to the creation of a personal political machine was the assumed political unreliability of the expatriate administrative cadres. Another was the lack of political control over the key points in the national economy. When political independence was obtained, the Prime Minister, as had been expected, did not gain control over the Ghanaian economy. Not only were export and import trade, banking, insurance, transportation, and communications essentially in expatriate (i.e., mainly British) hands, but the country's major source of foreign exchange, cocoa, was securely tied up in a maze of international financing, marketing, and processing arrangements. Policy and decision-making concerning Ghana's cocoa crop was centered in London, not Accra. The same was true of other primary products such as diamonds, gold, and timber. It seemed, in 1957, that, for some time to come, a Ghanaian government would not be master in its own house, and that, for many years, the country would be dependent on foreign marketing facilities, foreign sources of finance, and a foreign technical staff. Moreover, the prospects were for progressively increasing reliance on imports of high-cost capital and consumer goods.

In these circumstances, the newly installed African Prime Minister held relatively little economic, hence political, power. As in the case of his Nigerian colleague, Dr. Azikiwe, Nkrumah had to submit to a public inquiry when he did attempt to gain a greater degree of control over the economy.[13] For a man impatient to transform the structure of society and to seize total power, the lack of effective control over the bulk of the population outside the party structure, which was feeble enough, over his own cabinet, the civil service, and the courts, was a source of irritation and a constant spur to subterfuge, subversion, and eventual destruction of the bothersome, restraining constitutional order.

Of particular sensitivity to an ardently nationalist regime and to Nkrumah personally was the continuing direct and indirect presence of British influence in the principal security services—the army, the police, and the Criminal Investigation Department. Removal of foreign influences and development of a personal control system over these sensitive instruments of power was a matter of highest priority.

II

Kwame Nkrumah:
The Political Man

When Kwame Nkrumah returned to the Gold Coast late in 1947, the social revolution that was to sweep the colonial world toward independence in little more than a decade was already making itself felt. The social, economic, and psychological consequences of World War II and the combined intervention of the United States and the Soviet Union in the affairs of the colonial powers gave the social-revolutionary movements in Africa the impetus needed to initiate the attack on their colonial masters. Although it can be disputed whether Nkrumah's role in the Gold Coast's march to independence was as seminal and instrumental as he and his mythmakers suggest, there can be little doubt that he played a most significant role in the engineering and timing of his country's independence.

Few published accounts of Nkrumah's rise to power and of his life and works are of value to the political analyst. All too frequently, the authors are unable to view their subject with even a minimum of detachment. A common failing is either to overlook entirely obvious deficiencies in the man's character and conduct or to discount them on the grounds that the new regimes of Africa deserve sympathetic understanding and tolerance. Another defect is the tendency to confuse Nkrumah the carefully staged myth with Nkrumah the practical politician

19

and machine boss. Underlying much of "Nkrumahiana" is a curious assumption that the ascribed goals of the African social-revolutionary movement must also be the goals of Nkrumah and his political collaborators. Hortatory rhetoric is treated like a manual for the actual operation of the government of Ghana. Events not necessarily related to his political behavior are linked with his career. Frequently, Nkrumah is equated with Ghana; or the drab and on occasion unedifying reality of a common political struggle for survival is submerged in a sea of high-sounding ideological generalizations.[1]

Only with great caution can Nkrumah's own writings be used as sources on his political behavior, positions, and intentions. Passages dealing with his philosophy of government are fairly revealing, but other passages need to be carefully interpreted and read in the proper context, and most important, they must always be suspected of being works of propaganda, mythmaking, or of symbol manipulation. To a considerable extent, his books and his domestic policies were directed at audiences outside Ghana; generally he addressed himself to the politically conscious elements across the African continent and, in part, to succeeding generations. *Consciencism* and *Neo-Colonialism: The Last Stage of Imperialism* quite obviously were not written by Nkrumah. The former contains chapters most likely written by a professional philosopher; the latter takes positions in sharp conflict with policies that Nkrumah was desperately trying to implement at the time the book was published. Moreover, the research done for the second book bears the mark of a team effort; it was too involved and far too extensive to have been undertaken by a busy leader of an active revolutionary regime. There is evidence that Nkrumah was not fully aware of the practical implications of what he was supposed to have written.[2] If the literary efforts associated with his name reflect any facet of his personality, they reveal a schizophrenic attitude that leads him to pursue distant objectives without regard to his immediate problems.

To cite passages in Nkrumah's books as evidence of certain political practices in Ghana or of national intent is not valid. For his books are designed to conceal or to touch up, not to reveal, the author's personal weaknesses and deficiencies—in effect, most of the political man. His more intimate collaborators knew of Nkrumah's unpredictable, often unexplainable moodiness, his tendency to explode in fits of anger or scorn, and his occasional displays of cold brutality. Toward the end of his rule, these traits appear to have been exacerbated.

The roots of Nkrumah's political behavior are diffuse and beyond accurate definitive assessment. If an attempt is made, nevertheless, to assess his political personality, it is with the understanding that the effort must be incomplete and tentative.

Capability, Intellectual Background, and Motivations

Kwame Nkrumah was a moderately capable, highly volatile and energetic, somewhat professional, somewhat amateurish leader. On public record, he was affable, readily forgiving, decidedly humane. Guiding his conduct, there was undoubtedly a strong desire to correct the injustices wrought by the colonial powers in Africa—and in particular upon his people—and a vision, albeit somewhat darkly seen, that he could, by creating a new society in Ghana, correct the social evils he believed to have been developed over a thousand years of feudalism and capitalism. He undoubtedly had other virtues and probably no fewer than the normal share of weaknesses found in political leaders.

Whatever his qualities, he did not begin to approach the perfection, intellectual brilliance, personal integrity, and self-discipline attributed to him by the more ardent among his followers and by the Ghanaian press. He was neither a Lenin, a Gandhi, nor a Christ.

Nor was he capable of performing the miracles credited to him —by implication—by contemporary adherents of the school that sees in almost every emergent state an all-embracing and dedi-

cated social- and economic-development organism. Sweeping
theoretical generalizations based on the make-believe world created in Convention People's Party (CPP) literature or conjured
up in the daydreams of hopeful or conformist politicians and on
the oracular pronouncements of the "leader" himself too often
concluded that prescriptions of what Ghanaian society *ought* to
be were already being translated into practice.[3]

Nkrumah's formal academic training and his academic achievements, though not outstanding, can nevertheless serve as a model
for aspiring young Africans. Nkrumah deserves the fullest credit
—and so does Lincoln University in the United States which
aided him—for setting an outstanding example in effort and
motivation in pursuit of higher education.

It is not possible to know to what extent his academic training—mainly in the history of political thought, general history,
education, social philosophy, and theology—contributed to the
development of his political skills. In conversation, he likes to
refer to his training in political science, suggesting that it has
been of special relevance to his political performance and insight. This is most doubtful. If his formal education can be
deemed functionally relevant to his conduct of government in
Ghana, it is most probably with regard to his general intellectual
range and in particular to his considerable talents as a political
organizer and propagandist. His education equipped him with
a store of ideas, concepts, and phrases that enabled him to couch
the strategic and tactical requirements of continental, international, and domestic political-machine politics in impressive,
respectable-sounding and superficially appealing formulas. His
brief but intensive encounter with theology—he fleetingly considered entering the Jesuit Order and had preached on occasion—
may have affected his political behavior in a number of ways.
During the early stages of his public career, his campaign style
was reminiscent of Christian missionary ardor and techniques.
Later, his personality cult contained theological elements. So

did his exhortations to the party and the formulations of Nkrumaism.

More relevant to his political performance were, most likely, his numerous extracurricular contacts and activities in the United States and Great Britain. While in the United States, he seems to have been associated with several social and political-action organizations primarily devoted to achieving peace and racial equality. What one observer calls his "temporary sojourn in the British Communist Party" undoubtedly added considerably to his store of organizational know-how and dialectical skill, although the latter is not too highly developed.[4] Many indications suggest that a dominant influence was George Padmore, a West Indian Negro leader, writer, onetime agent of the Communist International, and ardent, indefatigable defender of the rights of Africans everywhere. Nkrumah himself cites, among other influences, Padmore and Marx, Marcus Garvey, Engels, Lenin, and Mazzini.[5] A rather admiring observer wrote: "Heroes and hero worship are of Nkrumah's very life; he speaks still of certain personalities from Marx and Hitler to Aggrey and Fraser of Achimota."[6] Dr. W. E. B. DuBois, the American scholar and Negro leader, ranks high among Nkrumah's heroes. So does Dr. Nnamdi Azikiwe of Nigeria.

Undoubtedly, the years spent in the United States and Great Britain do much to explain Nkrumah's extraordinary reliance for advice and personal friendship on a large group of Europeans and Americans, many of whom became members of his "court." Understandably, Negroes, including West Indians—or, as Nkrumah preferred to call them, Afro-Americans—predominated among the American groups. It is not possible to determine how much advice he accepted from whom, but it seems certain that his views on race relations in the United States were heavily influenced by embittered accounts from these sources, not a few of whom were self-exiles from the United States. Aside from Padmore, the group included the West Indian Dr. T. R.

Makonnen, Julian Mayfield (a pseudonym), and Dr. DuBois' widow, Shirley. Not an exile, the noted American sociologist Professor St. Clair Drake exerted a moderating influence as a friend. Aside from their strong feelings on race relations in the United States, all these advisers had one thing in common: Their ideological concerns extended considerably beyond Ghana.

This applied far more to the large British contingent of full- and part-time advisers, confidants, intimates, and *"aficionados."* Most prominent among those who resided in Ghana, or who had accepted nonresident appointments there, were Geoffrey Bing, Patrick Sloan, Erica Powell, D. N. Pritt, Alan Nunn May, Thomas Hodgkin, and Mr. and Mrs. Ron Bellamy. Exerting personal influence of one kind or another, primarily from abroad and either directly or through intermediaries, were Bertrand Russell, Fenner Brockway, Barbara Ward, and numerous lesser partisans of various aspects of the Nkrumah revolution.

Some members of this group, foremost among them Sloan and the Bellamys, appeared to be active Communists, representative of an even larger but less visible group of Party members who, by all appearances, had been "seconded" from various parts of the world, including Asia and Latin America, to base their operations temporarily upon this strategic spot in Africa. Some of these people enjoyed direct access to Nkrumah. Others worked on him through policy papers, speech-writing, and diverse other channels. All in all, these people were able to achieve degrees of influence in Ghana that they would scarcely have been able to match at home. Some of them were hard-bitten, cynical professional revolutionaries; others, like Sloan, appeared to be filled with nostalgia for the lost horizons of Lenin's Revolution, and now deluded themselves into seeing in Nkrumah a second coming, in Nkrumaist Ghana a second opportunity to create the society of their dreams. Many of them were concerned with matters quite unrelated to the vital interests of the Ghanaian people. Influential in various fragmentary ways—in politics, culture, law, science—and apparently independent, were advisers like the well-intentioned but politically naïve Thomas Hodgkin, his Nobel Prize-winning wife, Dorothy, and Dr. Alan Nunn May. Whether these foreigners wielded significant political influence or not, they undoubtedly constituted important, perhaps prime, sources of inspiration for the impressionable Ghanaian leader. More or less skillful articulators, with numerous international ties—Barbara Ward had direct access to two U.S. Presidents during the period of Nkrumah's rule—these people lent their prestige as well as their skills to provide guidance for Nkrumah, and to provide internationally respectable rationales (indeed, in some cases, excuses) for many of his moves and actions. Operating at various levels, Barbara Ward, Bertrand Russell, Fenner Brockway, and Thomas Hodgkin in particular assisted Nkrumah in his effort to cover up the intellectual nakedness of his rule.

In a category all by himself was Geoffrey Bing, former British MP, QC, who, it should be noted for the record, had come to Nkrumah after having enjoyed the confidence of Nkrumah's opposition. He appears to have regarded himself as an *eminence grise,* or perhaps as a socialist Robinson Crusoe tutoring politically inexperienced Africans in the high strategies of social-revolutionary world politics. There is no room for doubt as to Bing's range of influence upon Nkrumah, and he used Nkrumah as a foil to settle old scores on the British and world political scenes. Although he is not a Communist, his antipathies were rather one-sided: they were directed overwhelmingly against the West.

Partiality toward the Communists in the great international confrontation was generally a characteristic of most of the international representatives of the political Left whom one encountered on Ghanaian soil. If Nkrumah had an anti-Western tendency, it was reinforced and fed continuously from these sources. Far more eager to strike a blow for a world revolution of one kind or another than to assist the people of Ghana in their desperate plight, this group contributed substantially to the conversion of the Ghanaian seat of government into an alienated enclave on the coast of West Africa, directed more and more toward world revolutionary goals.

This group may have been partly responsible for the abandon with which Nkrumah plunged into pan-African affairs long before the Ghanaian base had been secured. Whereas Nkrumah originally may have believed that the liberation of Ghana would not be complete without the liberation of the rest of Africa, these partisans led Nkrumah into forgetting his more immediate concerns and responsibilities. As many Ghanaians pointed out with bitterness after Nkrumah's fall, the alienation of Kwame Nkrumah from his own people may well have been, in part, the responsibility of these non-African revolutionaries. They were assisted by the Soviets, the Chinese, and others who had no compunction about flattering Nkrumah into believing that he was the African instrument of the world revolution. All of this eventually produced a serious, perhaps fatal flaw in Nkrumah's political posture: a confusion of his immediate responsibilities toward Ghana with remote and, for him, unreal responsibilities. A schizophrenic political personality was created: Nkrumah's attention and energies were directed increasingly away from his home base and he therefore could do justice to neither his domestic nor his adopted continental constituency.

It is quite possible that another interpretation of Nkrumah's intellectual development brings us closer to an understanding of his motivation. As with many bright young Africans living under colonial rule, Nkrumah appears to have been drawn early to a course of rebellion against the old order. Spurred on by the advice and writings of such militants as Azikiwe of Nigeria, the young arrival at Lincoln University soon developed into an African freedom evangelist. His theological concerns, coupled with a gift of oratory, produced a fervor and an ardency which left many of his listeners impressed, if somewhat unconvinced. Gradually, through reading, learning, and discussions, a youthful vision was transformed into a flaming cause. The strident Africanism of a Marcus Garvey and the stinging, racially oriented taunts of a W. E. B. DuBois undoubtedly fed the flames. The rape of Ethiopia apparently affected Nkrumah deeply, as it affected black intellectuals everywhere. The event strengthened his conviction that a crime of enormous proportions was being committed against his African brothers and sisters, and that colonialism had to be terminated across the continent, as a matter of greatest urgency, within his lifetime.

Revulsion over the attack on Ethiopia—the oldest African state—romantic fervor, and further exposure to African lore persuaded him that a free and independent Africa was more than a dream: it was a reality, a thousand years old, concealed from the world by a veil of misinformation and propaganda spread by the colonial powers; it was a reality to be brought to light by the touch of a determined leader. But while he studied in the United States, the vision, or the cause, never assumed clearly defined dimensions. To many of his listeners, the young African enthusiast remained a rebel without arms, a charming Don Quixote out to conquer windmills, in battle against overwhelming odds.

Nkrumah did not have concrete revolutionary ideas until his arrival in London. It is quite possible that without the direct exposure to Communist dialectics, revolutionary strategy and tactics, and political cunning and deception—without the intimate contacts with George Padmore, Fenner Brockway, and generally with the militant wing of the Labour Party—the graduate of Lincoln Theological Seminary and the University of Pennsylvania would have pursued his legal studies and become, in time, one of Ghana's abler attorneys, or a journalist. He might have become a bourgeois who would have resisted with eloquence and determination some other dictator.

It was in London that the romantic notion of a free continent was transformed in Nkrumah's mind into a program of "positive action," to be executed by systematic, revolutionary tactics, dialectically consistent with the prescriptions of Lenin and Marx.

Nkrumah himself, in his Foreword to *Towards Colonial Freedom,* recalls: "It was not until I arrived in London in 1945 and came face to face with the colonial question, experiencing first hand the determination of student bodies fighting and agitating for colonial freedom in the very heart of the country that possessed a vast colonial empire, that I was stimulated to complete this book."[7] This book and the *Declaration to the Colonial Peoples of the World,* adopted at the Fifth Pan-African Congress held at Manchester in October, 1945, were the most poignant expositions of Leninist thought to come from the pen of Kwame Nkrumah.

Insights gained from exposure to Communist thought and dialectics suggested to Nkrumah that Africa was a continent seething with revolutionary longing and that nothing could prevent a determined and skilled leader from releasing and mobilizing the stored-up energy of the long suffering people. It may well be that when Nkrumah alighted upon the shores of the Gold Coast, he was looking beyond that comparatively small area to the liberation of the continent as a whole—the liberation of the Gold Coast to be the first step, the means to serve a greater end.

The moral disintegration of the idealist, the dedicated revolutionary, may have begun when he attempted the impossible: to run before he could walk. Preoccupied with distant goals, his eyes firmly fixed on the horizon, he failed to notice the traps beneath his feet. Perhaps *The Spark* was not so far off the mark when its editors noted: "From the very beginning Kwame Nkrumah has had an all-African perspective. However, he was forced by the naked facts of African political life to start his activities as a leader of the people in his own home country."[8] As it turned out, the naked facts of African political life in time proved to be his undoing.

As the grinding details of government and administration and the temptations presenting themselves to those in high office crowded in on the rather inexperienced leader, the romance of a continental freedom movement appeared ever more attractive. It is likely that the thought of seizing power in Ghana in order to achieve the greater goal of the liberation of Africa never left Nkrumah; but it gradually deteriorated into a form of escape, exhilarating and psychologically more rewarding than the drudgery of ever more disappointing experiences at home. At international conferences, the realities of political life could be put aside more readily than was possible when straining against the limits of a declining economy. When one discussed the eventual unity of a continent, complex social, economic, and military problems could be "solved" with a sweep of the hand or an elegantly advanced dialectical tour de force. The well-turned phrase was far more likely to win applause at a conference of African freedom fighters than at a meeting with financial advisers.

Perhaps sometime around 1960, it dawned on Nkrumah that he was not cut out to govern a country, to preside over the implementation of economic-development plans, to discriminate between competing prescriptions for economic progress, to struggle with budgets and myriads of reports, to make firm and binding decisions. But, if this was the case, by then he was trapped. Frustration, recriminations, and bitterness resulted from attempts to reconcile his conflicting interests—his need to maintain the ever more precarious seat of power at Accra and the desire to lead a free and united Africa. In the contest between the idealist commitment to African liberation and retention of power at home, the latter, of course, had to win out. The corruption and decline of Kwame Nkrumah may well have been the product of the clash between idealism and reality, at home and abroad, aggravated by basic human weaknesses of the man.

Although the succeeding chapters will deal with the nature of Nkrumah's commitment to Socialism from a variety of points of view, it is appropriate at this stage in the analysis to attempt to assess the degree to which Nkrumah believed in the Socialistic creed. The fact that Nkrumah was a practicing and accomplished private capitalist—in fact, by all appearances, an accomplished rogue in matters of finance—does not by itself negate the thesis that a Socialist Ghana may have been his goal. It is possible—though perhaps not moral—for a man to prescribe one social program for a country and at the same time deviate from the prescription in his personal conduct.

There can be little doubt that the Socialist philosophy as it was practiced in the Soviet Union appealed greatly to young African nationalists after World War II. Appropriately or not, Africa's future leaders found in the Soviet Union, and even more fundamentally in Leninism and in Marxism, a sympathetic understanding for their cause. Socialism and Communism were protest movements of the poor and oppressed, and the Africans were poor and oppressed.

Beyond the merely superficial affinity of kindred revolutionary movements, there was the more concrete aspect of political assistance and training. Furthermore, Socialism and Communism offered a formula for the destruction of "imperialist" control over the resources, hence the power structure, of the rising African states. Nkrumah never made a secret of his conviction that the liberation of Africa depended, in the first instance, on political action, and, in the second instance, on the nationalization of basic resources and the transfer of all economic control from foreign hands to the Africans themselves.

But Nkrumah lacked the ability to reconcile his ideals with reality, to develop a synthesis meaningful to the Ghana of his time.

Undoubtedly, Nkrumah's intellectual makeup and political personality are to some extent the product of cultural influences associated with his tribal origins; to sort out the analytically relevant aspects of these origins, however, and to relate them meaningfully to the political behavior of the mature man may be beyond the range of contemporary social-science methodology.

All of us, more or less, are still under the influence of ancient superstitions. However, Kwame Nkrumah seems to be extraordinarily superstitious. While it is certainly not my intention to elevate rumors to the level of historical fact, Nkrumah's behavior appears to have been more related to tribal superstitions and beliefs than would be indicated by the image of a modern, progressive, worldly leader. At any rate, it is difficult to discount the possibility that the political decisions of Kwame Nkrumah were not wholly detached from traditional customs. Two incidents reveal a glimpse of that less well-known side of Nkrumah.

When, in October, 1961, Nkrumah decided to drop his erstwhile friend and comrade, the onetime Minister of Finance Gbedemah, he instructed his foil in Parliament, Kofi Baako, to leave nothing unsaid that could destroy the image of the man. Accordingly, Baako confided to the Assembly, while holding two bags of "black powder" in his hands, that these bags represented juju—implements of sorcery—with which Gbedemah had attempted to kill him. Still referring to the peril from the black powder, Baako urged with great force and emotion that the House pass the Criminal Procedure Bill because it would protect the individual's liberty from such hazards. "The Bill," he said, "is for such people."[9] There was throughout Baako's address a suggestion that the magic powders had eventually been intended to be applied against the President himself.

The incident was indicative of the atmosphere in which Nkruumah lived, for no minister—Baako was a member of the cabinet at the time—would have dared to appear on the floor of the National Assembly with two bags of black powder in his hands and suggest what he did unless assured that the line of attack would be approved at the top.

After the coup, E. Ayeh-Kumi, financial and economic adviser and confidant of the President, revealed at a press conference another example of Nkrumah's reliance on supernatural forces. Nkrumah, as was his nature, had become suspicious of Ayeh-Kumi. Ayeh-Kumi related that on two occasions he was taken by a security officer to see a Muslim who "told me to open my palm, and he fumbled through sand and a mirror which he had in his hand and told me that the President liked me very much. I would have a great future if I would remain loyal to Kwame Nkrumah. He gave me some roots, including what appeared to be gum arabic, and incense to smoke once a week and a bottle of a mixture which was basically Florida water to rub my [body] and face before I go to work."[10] The Muslim, it appears, was a "marabout," or "holy man," from Kankan in Guinea whom Nkrumah had brought to Ghana for his personal use. Ayeh-Kumi continued: "Later I was informed that the old Mohammedan had died and his son had been installed in his place and was due to come to Ghana to reinvoke spirits on behalf of the deposed President and I should get ready as he wanted to see me also when he arrived."

Clearly, Nkrumah was a man of several worlds, possibly at peace with none.

All but a handful of giants among the political leaders of the world lack the intellectual resources and training to adjust to the ever-changing environment. Most are prisoners of obsolescent social philosophies and concepts, wedded to the prescriptions that brought them to power. Their concepts of the universe are static and thus they tend to be overtaken by events. Their "visions," with few exceptions, are in fact backward-looking, dealing with yesteryear's problems. This is particularly true of leaders who subscribe to rigid social doctrines. And there was no reason to believe that Nkrumah would manage to rise above this level of leadership.[11]

He certainly tried: reading voraciously, seeking the company of intellectuals—albeit self-seeking, flattering ones—he strove, to the best of his ability, to keep informed, improve his understanding of the changing world, and sharpen his skills of leadership. His mind was stocked with unassimilated ideas from political leaders, writers, philosophers, prophets, and charlatans; from Aristotle to Lincoln, from Jefferson to Mao Tse-tung, from Malcolm X to "holy men."

Like most leaders throughout the ages, Nkrumah was probably motivated, in the first instance, by the demands of "self." Social psychology suggests that where social restraints on the individual do not operate, are minimized, or can be effectively controlled by the individual, personal security and gratification become the dominant interests. There is no evidence that Kwame Nkrumah was an exception and much evidence that this generalization applies to him.[12] This is not to say that he lacked social consciousness or a sense of social commitment. It is merely focusing our attention—which has been clouded by many generalizations about systems, social dynamics, and political culture —on the distinction between the personal motivations of the leader and the aggregate interests of the society which he leads. Under a highly personalized form of government, considerations of the ruler's "self" are of paramount importance.[13]

Considerations of personal security consumed much of Nkrumah's time and energy. To secure his position of power, to control key points of power and influence in the country, and to watch over the movements of actual and potential rivals had to be the first order of business for the dictator. A substantial number of attempts were made on his life—at least three or four serious ones. These threats to his personal security did not emanate only from domestic sources. His foreign policies, overt and covert, constituted direct threats to the security of rulers in neighboring countries. He was positively obsessed by fear of the U.S. Central Intelligence Agency, an obsession constantly fed by operatives of other (primarily Eastern) intelligence services in his entourage as well as by the similarly motivated "advisers" from Western countries.

Nkrumah wished to attain prominence as the prime architect of African unity, to play a distinct historical role based not only on what he achieved in Ghana but also on what he could achieve on a continental scale.[14] This concept of his role in history appears to be patterned after Lenin.[15]

He has been described as living by "theory." It might be more useful to regard him as living by fragments of theories projected in oversimplified form onto a substantially unrelated and unreceptive world.

Very early in his career, while in London and in contact with the Communist Party, he engaged in efforts to lay the foundations for a Union of West African Socialist Republics, comprising both English- and French-speaking territories.[16] If he did not regard himself as another Lenin, Nkrumah most likely did see himself as the African leader whose historic mission and opportunity it was to bring Lenin's vision into being on the African continent.

Gandhi and Christ, the latter perhaps more in his secular, sociopolitical rather than his spiritual role, also appear to have served as models for Nkrumah's public posture. An editorial in *The Ghanaian Times* reflects Nkrumah's image of himself:

> The greater truth is that while Ghana is unquestionably Kwame Nkrumah, the man himself belongs to a scale far transcending the bounds of one nation, even of one continent and one race of people. He belongs to a whole historical epoch, rises with the fortunes and aspirations of whole multitudes of the world's peoples for whom life is one mighty struggle for survival. . . .
>
> If he has been linked in an indissoluble union with Ghana, it is only because *the historical process demands an attachment to specific zone of operations.* . . . Lincoln, Patrick Henry, and Jefferson have all ceased to belong to one nation.
>
> If this is correct, it is even more so of the Founder of the first socialist state, the great Vladimir Lenin. . . .
>
> By the light that Lenin lit in Petrograd, the rays of socialism have come to illuminate the paths of millions of the world's peoples. . . .
>
> Kwame Nkrumah too had to liberate the people of Ghana from the scourge of British colonialism, but the fire of liberation which he kindled did not burn in Ghana alone. It shone beyond and across the land mass of Africa, set ablaze a new fury which gnawed away the shackles of imperialism from the rest of the continent of Africa.[17]

Although aspects of his private life seem to belie it and although he has insistently denied it in personal conversation, his autobiography, occasional public utterances, and long-standing identification with a fundamentally race-oriented movement suggest that the element of race is not entirely missing as a motivating factor in his political conduct. No student of colonialism can fail to appreciate a black man's reaction to years of victimization under white rule. Moreover, the international situation appears increasingly to sharpen divisions along racial lines, and the actions of the frustrated African masses—to whom Nkrumah constantly appeals and whose leader he believes himself to be—take on increasingly a racist hue. Given the social pressures exerted upon him, the combination of interests and opportunities of his increasing political commitment, and the frustrations of his pan-Africanist aspirations, which he consistently and exclusively traced to the governments of Western countries, it seems entirely plausible that the "color-blind" Nkrumah—as he has described himself to visitors—would have turned into a racist in time.[18]

There are, of course, numerous additional sources of political behavior that might explain Nkrumah's political style and conduct. He seems to have regarded himself as *sui generis* among African leaders.

When it was revealed that the Nigerian Prime Minister Sir Abubakar Tafawa Balewa had been killed during the military coup in Nigeria in January, 1966, Nkrumah, with accustomed immodesty, broadcast to Africa that the Nigerian "had died a victim of forces he did not understand . . . in a struggle whose nature he never understood."[19] The implication was that Nkrumah did understand and that he did because he possessed the only keys to an understanding of these forces and the struggle—namely, the philosophical, analytical tools of "scientific socialism." His assessment of all other African leaders, without exception, was identical. Those who had been replaced and those who had not yet fallen were, according to him, all men of limited vision, mistaken opinions, and misplaced idealism. Conservatives like Félix Houphouet-Boigny of the Ivory Coast, Maurice Yameogo of Upper Volta, Hamani Diori of Niger, Leopold Senghor of Senegal—in fact, the entire group of pro-French leaders in French-speaking Africa—were relics of a political universe that had, in Nkrumah's view, long ceased to have any justification for existence.[20]

In Ghanaian press references, it often was "Nkrumah of Africa," while Kenyatta and Nyerere and Nasser were only identified by their respective countries. There was but one leader of Africa, and his name was Kwame Nkrumah. The first words of his will were: "I, Kwame Nkrumah of Africa . . . "

Nkrumah on Personal Power and Control

Although Nkrumah should not be regarded as the sole (possibly not even the principal) author of books and articles published under his name, he wrote sections in some of them, authorized publication of all of them, and probably edited the sections dealing with his private and public conduct. To an extent, therefore, these books are auxiliary sources of information and general guides to his personality, especially in the passages spelling out his personal role in the developing scheme of government.

Over the years, from *Towards Colonial Freedom* (1942–45) to *Neo-Colonialism: The Last Stage of Imperialism* (1965), his demands for absolute power became ever more strident and insistent, although formulated in terms related to the office of the presidency and to party control. One of the earliest manifestations of Nkrumah's desire for personal control is found in the document "The Circle," drafted by him in 1947.[21] The members of "The Circle"—a secret political core group—were pledged to "accept the leadership of Kwame Nkrumah," significantly in the context not only of Ghana but of West Africa and eventually of an all-African Union of Socialist Republics. The several constitutions of the Convention People's Party, carefully checked by him, also spell out in one way or another the same principle of absolute, unquestioned, personal control over the machinery of power.[22]

His autobiography (1957) contains the general outlines of what was to become the personal political machine:

> Capitalism is too complicated a system for a newly independent nation. Hence the need for a socialistic society. But even a system based on social justice and a democratic constitution may need backing up, during the period following independence, by emergency measures of a totalitarian kind. Without discipline, true freedom cannot survive.[23]

In *I Speak of Freedom*, published in 1961, the need for special measures is outlined:

> The first duty of government is to govern. Hence the preservation of our internal security is paramount. It is obvious that we are dealing with conditions quite unlike those in many countries. Thus we must adopt methods appropriate to the problems we have to solve and still preserve basic rights of the individual.[24]

In *Africa Must Unite*, published in 1963, under the heading "Bringing Unity in Ghana," the rationale for the liquidation of organized opposition, restriction of press and personal freedoms, and construction of a personal political machine is presented in terms of the threat posed by dissension stimulated by "imperialist" interests in a divided, unstable country. This dissension, revealingly enough, was said to focus on Nkrumah's personal conduct.

> How could our people pull their weight with zeal and dedication when it was ceaselessly being drummed into them that their government was unscrupulous, inept, and corrupt, that their leaders were venal and power-thirsty, and that the national effort was being invoked not for the greater glory of Ghana but for the personal glory of Kwame Nkrumah? This was not freedom of expression. This was

irresponsible license, and if allowed to continue unbridled, it could have undermined our state, our independence, and the people's faith in themselves and their capacities.[25]

Most noteworthy in this passage is the equation of "the people's faith in themselves and their capacities" with preservation of an unsullied image of their leader.

Having established the need to protect the personality of the leader from criticism, the distinction between head of state and head of government—i.e., between President and Prime Minister, was abolished in order to simplify the processes of government for the benefit of the people, who were said to insist that "primacy" was associated with "power."[26]

The position of a titular leader, merely signing acts of Parliament upon which he makes no impact, would not have been easy for [the people] to grasp, for it is a meaningless fiction *without content*. It is our hope that the system we have adopted, which combines the Premiership with the Presidency, will give stability and resolute leadership in the building of our country. In our opinion, it responds to the mood of our people and meets the exigencies of our actual situation. The reservation of certain powers to the President was felt to be necessary to allow opportunity for decisive action in pushing forward our development. [Italics added.][27]

Two omissions or falsifications stand out. The role of the head of state is misrepresented as being totally meaningless and purely ceremonial. Concealed from public view is the profound constitutional and political significance of the separation of powers between a head of state and a head of government. Also concealed are the objectives of total seizure of power by the President. "Reservation of certain powers to the President" is a gross understatement of what was really intended.

Still another rationale—namely, the extraction of surplus capital and labor—was cited as justification for concentrating power in the hands of one man:

Ghana has established a democratic structure employing the normal paraphernalia associated with such a governmental form, which is really ahead of our pre-industrial status. To have effective control over the rate of our development, we had to hold something in reserve. We had to trim our political coat to suit our social and economic cloth.

The increased authority given to the President is to enable him to exercise the positive leadership that is so vital to a country seeking to pull itself up by its bootstraps. . . . *There are some jobs in the world that can best be done by a committee; others need a managing director.* [Italics added.][28]

On the face of it, the position expressed appears to be quite reasonable. When closely examined, however, the analogy to the managing director who will conduct the affairs of the state, including extraction of reserves from the labor of the people, without benefit of advice from even a committee, reveals starkly the planned assault on the remaining aspects of constitutional government.

Not all of Nkrumah's public pronouncements were as pointedly directed toward the objective of seizure of total power. On occasion—alas, only prior to independence—he painted an entirely different picture. The best example of that posture—an extensive endorsement of the tenets of the liberal, democratic state—was his address in Parliament on November 12, 1956, on the motion to approve the independence constitution. But that address was the last of its kind, merely a reflection of the tactical requirements of the moment.[29]

III

Building the Political Machine (I)

THE CONSTITUTIONAL AND POLITICAL SITUATION AT INDEPENDENCE

Since this study deals in substance only with the period begining after March 6, 1957, when Ghana became independent, a brief survey of the pre-independence constitutional and political situation is in order.

Constitutionally, the Prime Minister's powers were circumscribed by several restraints.[1] The Governor-General, as representative of the Queen, was empowered to veto legislation passed by the Ghanaian Parliament that was unacceptable to him on constitutional grounds. The courts, backed by a provision that made the British Crown's Privy Council the highest court of appeal, could—and in some respects did—exercise a restraining influence on the executive branch of the government. As a member of Parliament, the Prime Minister, along with his Ministers, was expected to submit regularly to the popular controls exercised in free and secret elections. Certain basic rights and freedoms were guaranteed by the constitution. There also were regional assemblies set up in response to demands by the opposition parties. These bodies were designed to bring regional interests to bear on the central government and to slow down, if not prevent, expansion of central-government powers at the expense of the several regions.[2]

Administratively, the Prime Minister was hemmed in by a number of expatriate Permanent Secretaries occupying key control

41

posts in certain Ministries. More generally, he was surrounded by politically neutral—or in the opposition, depending on one's point of view—Ghanaian civil servants, the majority of whom he suspected of identifying themselves with the anti-Nkrumah opposition.[3]

Nkrumah's party, the Convention People's Party, controlled 72 of the 104 seats in the National Assembly, only 7 seats short of the three-fourths majority needed to effect a formal constitutional change. In the National Assembly, the opposition, though heavily outnumbered, constituted a visible and therefore irritating source of personal embarrassment to Nkrumah. Its front bench, weighted rather heavily with intellectual and oratorical capability, time and again routed Nkrumah's colorful, resolute, but less articulate spokesmen in debate and during technical arguments. Fundamentally strongest among the opposition parties was the National Liberation Movement (NLM), a coalition of tribal elements, mainly Ashanti, and of professionals and intellectuals; the latter groups set party policy, while the former constituted the main source of funds and grass-roots election support. The NLM posed a serious extraparliamentary threat as did the entire Ashanti region, the source of the major share of Ghana's export earnings, controlled by Ghana's socially most cohesive and compact, best-administered, and politically most aggressive tribal organization.[4]

The Northern People's Party (NPP), although credited with control of a few more seats than the NLM, was organizationally feeble, financially impotent, and led by comparatively inarticulate, traditional elements from the poorest regions, the Northern Territories. It did not pose a serious threat to Nkrumah's designs. Neither did the other relatively insignificant religious, tribal, and regional splinter groups. If the latter troubled Nkrumah at all, it was because of their potential value as rallying points for tribal and sectional agitation and, from his point of view, subversion. He was never able to shed his suspicions of the Ga people in this respect.[5]

How did Kwame Nkrumah reach the plateau from which he

was able to embark upon the conversion of an entire state into a personal political machine?

Professor W. Arthur Lewis, onetime economic adviser to Nkrumah, provides us with a useful, though somewhat hyperbolic, thumbnail sketch of Nkrumah's rise to power. Examining the reasons why "radical parties" were established in certain African states once the independence movement had gotten under way, he notes that "the explanation in each case turns on personalities":

> In Ghana, the explanation is accidental. There was an active political movement, going back fifty years, run by the middle classes with the support of some powerful chiefs. Its leader in 1947 was Dr. Danquah, lawyer, and brother of a Paramount chief. The movement decided that the time had come to organize a mass political party. Ako Adjei, a lawyer, son of a trader, had met Kwame Nkrumah in London and had been impressed by his oratorical and administrative gifts. He therefore suggested to Danquah that Nkrumah, who had been away for ten years, should be brought back and made organizing secretary of the party. Danquah agreed to do this, in complete ignorance of Nkrumah's opinions. Nkrumah came back, and using the money and prestige of the movement and the protection of the chiefs, built up a mass movement throughout the southern half of Ghana. He built it, however, on a basis of personal loyalty to himself, and endowed the younger members with the radical ideas which he picked up during his temporary sojourn in the British Communist Party. When the movement realized what was happening, they deprived Nkrumah of his office. But it was then too late. He took the mass movement with him, and it could not be recaptured.[6]

A general, rather perspicacious commentary on Nkrumah's march to power and an appropriate introduction to a discussion of the building of the political machine is found in Elspeth Huxley's assessment written in 1954:

> Dr. Nkrumah's rise is something new in Africa, not because he seeks power—there is nothing at all new in that—but because the ways

in which he has gained and now holds it are alien. African tribes had evolved, before the European advent, an elaborate and most effective system of curbing the abuse of power by their rulers through councils, elders, and priests. All this has gone by the board. As yet, Africa has no technique for curbing people like Dr. Nkrumah. He has the ball at his feet. With a few Western-trained, ambitious men at the centre, and at the periphery a mass of rather credulous and unsophisticated persons whose age-old social structure is in rapid decay, there seems to be no limit to what can be done.[7]

Although Miss Huxley overstated Nkrumah's freedom of movement, she and a few others perceived at that early stage the shape of things to come.[8]

SECURITY, COERCION, AND CONTROL

Initial Measures

Hitler used the burning of the German national Parliament building, the *Reichstag*, to ring down the curtain on the constitutional order and launch a totalitarian society. What was Nkrumah's launching point? As noted above, there was evidence that the British Governor and the circles he represented had already written off the possibility of actually creating an open society, a working, pluralist democratic state. However, such a state had been fashioned on paper, and the new African regime, as well as its British sponsors, were at least for a time committed to honor some of its features. Certainly, public opinion in Britain, particularly in circles associated with the Labour Party, could be counted on to protest against any blatant interference with constitutionally guaranteed rights and the rule of law—e.g., *habeas corpus* and due process of law. The British press and of course Parliament—the legal godfather of the Ghanaian constitution—were keenly attuned to and ready to pounce on any acts suggesting violation of basic human rights or minority interests, or the establishment of a dictatorship. For those and other reasons—e.g., continued dependence on foreign investment—the moves to convert the bothersome paper democracy into an outright system of authoritarian rule, backed up by "emergency measures of a totalitarian kind," had to be camouflaged as efforts to protect individual rights and freedoms, to guarantee law and order, national unity, and stability.[9]

It has been suggested that Nkrumah's launching point was provided by the noisy, raucous protest movement of the Ga-Dangbe tribal group living in and around Accra. Although the movement had been established prior to independence, demonstrations in mid-1957, the possible seeds of insurrection, furnished Nkrumah with the excuse to introduce more severely repressive measures than were sanctioned under the prevailing statutes. Moving swiftly, the Secretary General of the Party, Cecil Forde, declared on August 13, 1957: "Perhaps there may be much to be said for a temporary dictatorship than a democratic state (sic) where the Opposition is violent, waspish and malignant."[10]

To engineer the conversion to a system of personal rule, Nkrumah called upon the member of his cabinet who was most loyal, least scrupulous about democratic principles, least informed, and toughest-minded: Krobo Edusei. Attached to the pugnacious Minister for general guidance and to provide the legal rationale for personal rule in a form most palatable to public opinion, especially in Britain, was a barrister, Geoffrey Bing, onetime legal adviser to the opposition groups he now was called upon to "legislate" out of existence.[11]

The conversion started with attempts to win over some opposition leaders by offering them posts in a national "coalition" government. Among those singled out were those leaders who had defected from the CPP in 1954—the foremost among them being Joe Appiah, Victor Owusu, E. K. Kurankyi-Taylor, and William Ofori Atta. Simultaneously, on August 23, a Deportation Act was passed, purportedly to secure the deportation of two Nigerians but actually to intimidate the weakest links in the opposition chain—namely, aliens and those whose claims to Ghanaian citizenship could not be supported by conclusive evidence. The law was aimed mainly at the substantial group of Moslems, especially those from Nigeria, who made up one of the principal ethnic and religious elements in the opposition. This was followed by the Avoidance of Discrimination Act of December, 1957, which, on the surface, only outlawed all parties based on "religious" considerations but actually struck at all bases of operation for an effective opposition. Recalcitrant chiefs were intimidated by threats of removal—that is, destoolment. This was easily achieved by invoking or threatening to invoke any number of a great variety of legal provisions available to the regime—e.g., statutes related to "corrupt" practices. Since most appointments of chiefs under the colonial regime and thereafter had been made in a haze of legal ambiguities, the institution of chieftaincy proved to be a mere paper barrier to the conversion of the system to personal rule.

What appeared to be "measures taken to emphasize and augment the power of the party in the regions"[12] in reality were measures designed to secure Nkrumah's personal control over developments throughout the country. For example, it mattered very little that the newly appointed regional commissioners were all members of the CPP. The party possessed no independent power. Aside from the party leader, there existed no center, no source of power, controlling their conduct. Thus, under the guise of staffing the posts provided for in the 1957 constitution for the purpose of guaranteeing a modicum of decentralization in the government, Nkrumah planted the seeds of the personal political machine throughout the regions. He selected and appointed the commissioners, remained personally in touch with them, controlled their emoluments, and decided when and on what grounds they were to be disciplined. The stipulations for appointment included the provision that those selected were to be personally and directly responsible to the government. One glance at who the government was revealed the true nature of the appointments and the place the appointees were to hold in the developing power and influence structure.

The regional assemblies provided for in the 1957 constitution were also promptly converted to the service of the personal political machine. The colonial administration, which had negotiated the inclusion of provisions for election to these assemblies, had no reason to believe that honest elections could be conducted in Ghana. Thus, no one could seriously have believed that these assemblies would live up to the expectations of their democratic, federalist-minded designers. Not surprisingly, they were promptly and easily brushed aside. First, all five regional assemblies were captured by the CPP, a process made easier when the opposition boycotted the regional elections. Each of the firmly controlled assemblies then passed a bill clearing the way for its own speedy demise.[13] The death warrant was duly approved by two-thirds of the National Assembly, the CPP bloc having been enlarged by induced defections from the opposition.

Among the remaining potential sources of resistance to arbitrary personal rule were the courts and the legal profession in general. To brush aside the courts or to reach dramatically into the potential hornets' nest of the international fraternity of jurists did not seem politic at the moment. For one thing, there was the ever-watchful House of Commons. Also, private investors, whose assistance was still valued, were known to shy away from countries whose governments subscribed openly to arbitrary rule. Last but not least, legal technicians advised Nkrumah that direct political intervention at that stage, would most probably raise havoc with the sensitive, intricate juridical machinery in Ghana itself. Yet the requirements of the political machine would not tolerate compromise or mutual accommodation in matters deemed essential to political survival. Accordingly, Parliament was directed to legitimatize, by formal approval, additional repressive measures.[14]

Taken altogether, these established the supremacy of political power over the force of law. From the point of view of personal power over lives, property, and political behavior, the

most crucial, most far-reaching measure of coercion was the
Preventive Detention Act of 1958. Nominally, it was the Governor-General who, under the Act, "may order the detention
of any person who is a citizen of Ghana if satisfied that the order
is necessary to prevent that person acting in a manner prejudicial
to the security of the state."[15] In practice, it was the Prime
Minister who had to be "satisfied," and his perception of threats
to the security of the state centered on threats to the "leadership of Kwame Nkrumah," as had been laid down quite explicitly in the document called "The Circle." To facilitate political control over the legal apparatus, in the interest of "state
security," the Constitution (Amendment) Act of 1959 transferred the office of Attorney General from the public-service
category to that of a political appointee directly responsible to
Nkrumah.[16]

Under the Detention Act, Nkrumah could remove from circulation without publicity of any kind any person whom he
had reason to suspect of disloyalty—the proviso that the names
of detainees were to be published in the *Gazette* was largely
ignored in practice—and detain him for five years; and all this
without any formal appearance in court and without the right
of appeal to the courts. Again, this and related measures had
the appearance of general legislative defense against "activities
detrimental to the interests of state and society." The actual
implementation of these laws and the operation of the coercive
apparatus established under them, however, was under the control and supervision of neither state, society, nor even party
organs, but was exclusively under Nkrumah's control. Here was
the real fount of power and control in Ghana. The threat of
this legislation hung over the heads of the party functionaries
as heavily as it did over the heads of the nonparty segments
of the state.

Fortunately for Ghana and for Nkrumah's personal safety,
he displayed a sense of moderation and humane consideration
in the exercise of his ever-growing power. To some extent, his

moderateness was dictated by the requirements of Ghana's economy, which was rapidly approaching a crisis situation, and by his designs for Africa in general. Ghana was still a member of the sterling bloc and continued to depend upon Western (primarily British and U.S.) financial support as well as Western sources of supply and training facilities for students, public servants, police and army officers. He continued for the time being to heed advice from friends and long-time admirers and associates such as Bertrand Russell and Fenner Brockway, several British businessmen, and certain leaders of the American Negro movement. Also, as a member of Her Majesty's Privy Council, Nkrumah was not yet prepared to part company with the dignified assemblage of moderates in the British Commonwealth.

However, it is in the nature of repressive measures that the imposition of one inexorably begets the imposition of ever more stringent security measures. Moderate or not, Nkrumah had mounted a tiger when he embarked upon a course of constructing a personal, maximum-security apparatus.

The next round was ushered in with the formal removal of the anachronistic, and to Nkrumah unbearable, façade of the constitutional monarchy, and more generally, with the discarding of the by then meaningless independence constitution.

The 1960 Republic Constitution and Its Demise

The conducting of a "plebiscite" on a new constitutional document was a mere formality.[17] The outcome was a foregone conclusion. The issues presented by the government were wholly unrelated to the real issues at stake. No regime would come out and ask the people whether they wished to be governed indefinitely by a personal political machine. Instead, the public was asked to vote on social welfare, prosperity, employment, and so forth. The actual electoral exercise was farcical.[18] The opposition fielded a candidate against Nkrumah, his erstwhile employer, the noted barrister and scholar Dr. J. B. Danquah. But their candidate could not make himself heard, let alone seen, in most parts of the country, and his partisan supporters could not secure access to all polling places.

The new republic constitution further entrenched the personal political machine. It combined the position of Head of State, until then filled by the Queen, with that of Prime Minister in the new office of President, reminiscent of executive presidents in the United States and elsewhere. It endowed the "first President" with powers that enabled him, whenever he considered it to be in the "national interest" to do so, "to give direction by legislative instrument."[19] Since Nkrumah was lifetime chairman of the (for practical purposes) only political party operating in Ghana—a party that was guaranteed a majority in Parliament regardless of its conduct or policies—this provision had the effect of merging the executive and legislative functions of government, reducing Parliament to an appendage of the personal political machine for the duration of Nkrumah's rule.

The new constitution further assured personal supremacy in politics by a proviso that, for the purpose of giving special directive powers to Nkrumah, "the first President's initial period of office shall be taken to continue until some other person assumes office."[20] There being already an extremely low probability that some other person would assume office "constitutionally," "initial period" meant indefinitely. No student of politics should have difficulty in assessing the over-all impact of these provisions on the power and influence structure in Ghana and on political loyalties. There were the usual references to "the people," to "elections," and to other customary features of constitutional government, but most of these were purely diversionary.

The problem of the civil service was tackled in the by then accustomed manner: "Subject to the provisions of the Constitution and save as is otherwise provided by law, the appointment, promotion, dismissal, and disciplinary control of members of the public services is vested in the President."[21] Any influence that the Civil Service Commission could have exercised was eliminated, since neither "law" nor the constitution offered effective restraints. The civil service was, if not incorporated into the political machine, certainly sensitized to its demands.

Also brought under personal rule was the judicial service. The Judicial Service Act of 1960, passed by the subservient Constituent Assembly—convened to draft the 1960 document—made the President the appointing authority for all posts in the judicial service and the disciplinary authority for circuit judges and district magistrates. The republic constitution vested in the President the exclusive power to appoint all judges of the superior courts. Although there was a nominal requirement that removal action against judges of the Supreme Court or High Court be submitted to Parliament, the presidential control over that body was such that the constitutionally stipulated two-thirds majority could easily be obtained.[22] In effect, judges were deprived of security of tenure in all judicial acts in conflict with Nkrumah's political interests.

The President could henceforth legislate, administer, regulate; he could manipulate Parliament as he saw fit, override the "Standing Orders of the House," govern the conduct of all but a minute portion of its membership. Parliament was cowed by the simple device of lifting or threatening to lift the immunity of its members. This particular leverage had been incorporated in the National Assembly (Disqualification) Act of 1959, which provided that no person should be qualified for election to Parliament if a Preventive Detention Order was in force against him or had been in force at any time within five years preceding the election. The seat of a Member of Parliament was to be declared vacant if an order under the Preventive Detention Act was issued against him. These provisions were retroactive, enabling Nkrumah to remove from Parliament certain members of the Opposition against whom orders had been issued prior to passing of the Act.

The following exchange on the floor of the National Assembly, on August 24, 1960, was one of the last convulsions of a dying parliamentary system.

Mr. Joe Appiah (for the opposition, addressing the Speaker) : "I should like to ask, since you are the protector of the liberties of this House, by what authority a Member of Parliament was arrested by the police and taken into custody when Parliament is still sitting?"

Mr. W. A. Amoro (for the government) : "If a Preventive Detention Order is made against any Member of the House, he ceases to be a Member of Parliament."

Mr. P. K. K. Quaidoo (for the government) : "Mr. Speaker, as far as I remember, Members of Parliament enjoy immunity within the precincts of and inside this House. The Honorable Member for Atwima Amansie [Mr. Appiah] knows that the Honorable Member was arrested outside the precincts of this House. I do not think the immunity of Members of Parliament should be used as a cloak to protect or shield any Member whose act is prejudicial to the security of the state."

The Speaker then stated that had he known that the member in question, Mr. I. Asigri, had been detained under the Preventive Detention Act, he would not have allowed the question to be asked.[23]

The lessons to be drawn from that exchange could not possibly have escaped the attention of the numerically insignificant but dauntless group in Parliament whose critical faculties had not yet been extinguished. Clearly, no power in Ghana could protect a Member whose continued liberty was not, as the Preventive Detention Act put it euphemistically, "in the best interest of the public good." If criticism had to be voiced, one had to take care that it was directed far and away from the real center of power, away from the person, public conduct, and policies and decisions of the President. Learned arguments to the contrary, there were, in realistic political terms, no substantive limits to Nkrumah's powers in the 1960 constitution.[24]

A series of measures amounting to constitutional changes were promptly passed by ordinary legislation by the docile Parliament, further widening the powers allocated to the President. The Presidential Affairs Acts and its successive amendments, the Emergency Powers Act of 1961, and the Public Order Act of the same year, throttled surviving freedom of movement, public meetings, and processions, muzzling whatever opposition elements were left. Gradually, even the trappings of parliamentary democracy were removed, and the new constitution, barely promulgated, was reduced to a scrap of paper. The voters who had approved the republic constitution had provided Nkrumah with the springboard for the next leap, to a personal monopoly of power.

Protecting the Person and the Office of the President.

One particular set of measures deserves special attention. It is reminiscent of the maxim upon which Mussolini based his rule—*"Il Duce ha sempre ragione"* ("The leader is always right"). Or, to recall a concept related to French monarchs, one is reminded of lese majesty. Under a 1961 amendment to the Criminal Code, it became a criminal offense to undertake *anything* that would make the President an object of hatred, ridicule, or contempt.[25] The amendment might have seemed to some fair enough. But when viewed in the light of the ever more apparent fact that the President and the government and the whole administration were inextricably part of one political machine, it was clear that it empowered the government to interdict all forms of criticism of substantive government activities deemed contrary to "public policy"—i.e., contrary to Nkrumah's interests. In effect, the amendment raised the person and the activities of the President in all respects, official and unofficial, above all criticism.

During the desultory debate in Parliament on the pending bill, the Minister of Defense and Leader of the House, Kofi Baako, revealed the true intent of the measure in reply to a suggestion by the former Minister of Finance and of Health, the disgraced Gbedemah, that the bill distinguish between the President as Head of State and the President as Head of Government in order to "permit free criticism of government policies in Parliament."[26] Kofi Baako replied that those who wished to make a distinction between Head of State and Head of Government wish to "abuse this man [Nkrumah]" and "allow us to bring him into hatred, ridicule, or contempt as Head of Government." He proceeded to invoke the Akan tradition that, he said, combined in the chief the functions of ceremonial head of state and executive head of state, and claimed that the people in the 1960 referendum had "asked that the President should be both Head of State and Head of Government," and that in particular the people had, in Article 10 of the republic constitution, provided a "declaratory reason" for considering "our present President as a *special case* [italics added]." "There is this declaratory reason that this man as one man has the confidence of the people of this country, and has been doing whatever he can do within his human limitations to build up the country and also to free and unite Africa in concert with other African leaders."[27]

Kofi Baako, still referring to the 1960 constitutional referendum, which had simultaneously elected the National Assembly, concluded with a remarkable legal tour de force:

> Therefore, when after the referendum we were brought here by the constituents as a result of the referendum, we had in fact been given the mandate by the people to take steps to ensure that the essence and spirit of the Constitution is not in any way mutilated during the course of the implementation of our Constitution. It is for this reason that Members of Parliament gave special powers to the Head of State as Head of Government.[28]

The Minister of Justice, W. Ofori Atta, also referring to the alleged traditional roots of the office of President, wound up the debate with the crowning observation that "therefore, the Head of State of Ghana is a *sacred* person, irrespective of the party to which he belongs. [Italics added.]"[29]

Thus it was established by law and in effect made a constitutional amendment that Nkrumah was always right and that any oral or written criticism of him or of any of his acts or policies or those of his government for which he was responsible in totality would be deemed lese majesty and punishable as a criminal offense.[30]

An indication of the urgency that the government attached to the steady accrual of power to the President, and incidentally a measure of the degree of freedom left to Parliament, emerged during the debate on the Criminal Procedure (Amendment) Bill of 1961. The bill proposed, in effect, to empower the President to take certain offenses out of the jurisdiction of the district magistrates and have them tried, on the initiative of the Attorney General, in a Special Criminal Division of the High Court. The significance of this proposal was that proceedings before the Special Division could not be appealed except in cases involving Presidential pardon—and that trial by jury was excluded. In introducing this bill, which would seriously weaken the legal system, the Minister of Interior, Kwaku Boateng, warned: "It is my contention, Sir, that anybody who makes a statement to cast a shadow of doubt on the meaning of the Bill should forever be considered the most insidious enemy of our country. Those who are responsible for the national security must be the sole judges of what the national security requires."[31] "Those responsible" referred, of course, to Nkrumah and the security service, which he controlled.

The most critical section of the bill was exceedingly ambiguous. It not only gave the President power to transfer cases from one judicial level to another but also enabled him to define new crimes not covered by the Criminal Code. Ominously, the bill provided that the jurisdiction of the Special Criminal Division was to extend to "offenses specified by the President by legislative instrument."[32]

Thus, by the end of 1961, Nkrumah was free to rule by fiat through a controlled Parliament, to reach into the judicial structure at will, and to remove from the courts cases that he considered to be of security interest. With the aid of the 1958 Preventive Detention Act, he could reach anybody—including leaders of the party and Members of Parliament—who dared to criticize him or to complain about his public or private conduct. His person had been declared above the law, beyond criticism, sacred.

Extending the Security Web

Much of the security legislation could be understood in light of the problems faced by a government intent on rapid development, forced savings, industrialization, and alterations in production and consumption habits. Nkrumah had personal enemies, his policies had brought hardship to families of detainees and to the middle class in general, and he had purged or elbowed aside a number of party leaders. There had been several attempts on his life, and each incident provoked increased fears for his personal safety. What is significant in the context of this study is the steady increase of Presidential power that resulted from these security measures, even those not designed for that purpose. Legislation to protect Ghana from spies and other subversive agents of foreign governments is a case in point.

In 1962, the State Secrets Act was passed. Section 2 of that Act innocuously provided:

> Any address, whether within or without Ghana, reasonably suspected of being an address used for the receipt of communications intended for an agent of a foreign power, or any address at which such an agent resides, or to which he resorts for the purpose of giving or receiving communications, or at which he carries on any business, shall be deemed to be the address of an agent of a foreign power and communications addressed to the address to be communications with the agent.

This provision, combined with exhortations in the daily press that all opposition in Ghana was linked to foreign powers, especially Western "imperialist powers," covered the country with a blanket of fear. In that campaign, the CIA was a prime target. There is reason to believe that Nkrumah found the CIA scare a most effective foil in preventing consolidation of an internal opposition.[33] Persons singled out by the press for criticism, persons said or believed to be *persona non grata* to the President, came to be especially conscious of the implications of this legislated xenophobia. A curtain of silence was drawn around the "suspects," and social ostracism followed. The President could be assured of a minimum of contact among actual or potential opposition elements.

In June, 1962, the government moved to extend the Preventive Detention Act (PDA) beyond the five-year limit originally voted by Parliament. The new bill was intended to allow the government to keep in custody continuously any person originally detained under the 1958 Act. The memorandum accompanying the bill stated that the extension was "to enable the continuance of this Act without need for periodic resolutions of the National Assembly."[34] Clearly, the aim of this proposal was not conservation of the energies of Parliament. To pass a resolution every five years, or every ten, or every twenty—it was in Nkrumah's power to extend the period as he saw fit—would not consume much of the National Assembly's time. The real purpose was to prevent, once and for all, repetition of embarrassing moments in Parliament when complaining members brought to light the more sordid and clumsy administrative dimensions of the PDA.

During debate on the proposed extension, even the political midwife of the original Act, former Minister of Interior Krobo Edusei—by then himself suspect—was moved to complain that "anybody can go and cause the detention of anybody."[35] Taking advantage of the last remaining chance to voice criticism of the security program, the leader of the forlorn opposition group, Mr. Dombo, brought to light the intimate connection between the preventive-detention powers and the requirements of personal rule. He called attention to the case of a man who "happened to say [in conversation with a friend] that the doctoral degree of the President was not academically acquired but that it was conferred on him. As a result of what this man said, he was sent to the Court on the charge of having abused the President. Later on, that case was withdrawn from the Court and the man was detained."[36]

This case also illustrates that in practice the instrumentalities available to the President under the various Criminal Code and Criminal Procedure provisions, the provisions of the PDA, the "Presidential Affairs" legislation, and other laws were being employed interchangeably. In fact, the criminal, civil, and political facets of security policy had now been merged. They were now part of the same control structure.

The debate, or rather discussion, on the government bill revealed the extent to which government by law had been replaced by government by one man. As the PDA had developed in practice, it had reduced a sizable portion of the Ghanaian judicial system to mere farce.[37] The accused could not question the grounds on which he was being detained. These grounds could be no more than a suspicion on the part of a security official that the accused's continued freedom of movement was not in the best interest "of the public good." And the "public good," as stated explicitly in the Act, was what the President, the sole judge in each case, thought it was. "Where the President was satisfied," so the phrase went, a man could be detained indefinitely. Normal safeguards against judicial error were not part of the security legislation; all depended on the assumed "humanitarianism" of the President, or more important, on the chance that the details of a miscarriage of justice came to the attention of the President, that he was not too busy, that he listened to the right people, that the right person had last had his ear.

As for the extent to which the National Assembly could be counted on to take action against abuse of statutory powers by or in the name of the President, the fact that Members of Parliament could also be reached by Preventive Detention, in violation of standing orders, customs, and traditions, spoke powerfully in favor of discretion on their part.[38]

The Security Service Act of 1963 established a "Security Service as one of the Public Services of the Republic which shall be responsible directly to the President."[39] Section 6 provided that "no proceedings shall be instituted against the Republic in any Court in respect of anything done in accordance with the provisions of this Act and the Rules made thereunder." Although such provisions are common in other countries, it must be remembered that by 1963 there were in Ghana no other review bodies or checks on the Security Service that could be regarded as independent of the chief executive and his political-control system.

It appears that the command elements of the Security Service taking over the political and military security responsibilities from the British-trained Criminal Investigation Department were to a considerable extent trained in the Soviet Union and by Russian and East European specialists in Ghana.

Administratively, the Security Service was exclusively at the disposal of the President, completely independent from the party, the Central Committee of the party, the cabinet, the armed forces, and the police. It was meant to be the backbone of the personal political machine.

In December, 1963, the Prison Department was reconstituted into an autonomous Prisons Service by passage of the Prisons Act of 1963. Under the Act, prisons were placed directly under the President. This included the camps established especially to accommodate detainees under Preventive Detention.

Also in December, 1963, in response to a verdict by the Criminal Division of the High Court that the President disapproved of—and for which the Chief Justice was dismissed—the President was empowered by executive instrument to declare a decision of the court to be of no effect. In that event, other legislation ap-

plied and the person or persons affected could then be reached
by any of the remaining arms of presidential "justice."[40]

Routinely, all the foregoing and some of the succeeding security measures further enhancing the President's powers were initiated allegedly in response to disturbances, bombings, and several assassination attempts. However, all measures necessary to
combat actual—as distinct from imagined, alleged, or anticipated
—attacks on the state, its organs, its property, or the person of
the President, to ferret out the persons responsible, to try and
to convict them, and to take them out of circulation for long
periods of time were already on the statute books before Preventive Detention was introduced.

Tying Up Loose Ends

On January 2, 1964, still another attempt apparently was made
on Nkrumah's life. The circumstances surrounding this attempt
were obscure. Genuine or not, the incident was used to tighten
the security net still further. The top ranks of the police were
purged, the police substantially disarmed, and communication
channels within the police reoriented to tie in with the personal
political machine—i.e., more officers were encouraged to communicate directly with the President concerning security matters. Physical security measures at the official residence, Flagstaff House, were further tightened, new security construction
rushed, and the military-security contingent constantly near the
President and on the alert was numerically increased. The President's movements were henceforth more carefuly concealed and
managed in such a way as to render virtually unpredictable to
all but himself their timing, route, direction, and means of
transportation.

Shortly thereafter, in January, 1964, the by then wholly farcical electoral machinery was operated once more to place the
stamp of legitimacy on the liquidation of all formal opposition
in Ghana. Under a constitutional amendment "voted by the
people" in what was termed a referendum, the powers that had

theoretically remained with the people—according to the letter of the rapidly decaying constitutional document—were now fully transferred to the lifetime chairman of the sole remaining, now constitutionally recognized, "national party." Ironically, at the very moment when the last, already faint vestiges of popular control of the executive were laid to rest, the revised constitutional document increased the accent on the people as "the source of power and the guardians of the state."[41] Similarly, at a time when the personal machine was firmly entrenched in the legal and political web of government, the CPP was extolled as "the vanguard of the people in their struggle to build a socialist society" and as "the leading core of all organizations of the people."[42] The party qua party, of course, had been stripped of all power, potentialities, and initiative as thoroughly as the rest of the state apparatus.

As the actual power of the party was curbed, the volume of noise accompanying public references to its allegedly key role in state and society was steadily increased. In part, this was done to drown out protests against the loss of power by the people and Parliament, in part to drown out and overcome the more embarrassing manifestations of the personality cult.

Still, for "party" one had to read "personal political machine." The 1964 constitutional amendment had not, as was believed by somewhat gullible observers, ushered in the "one-party state." It had legalized the political machine of which the tattered organizational shell of a party was but one of several parts, carefully hedged in, meticulously controlled and inhibited, and thoroughly pruned of all vestiges of political independence. The members and the functionaries of the "vanguard" were as much under the thumb of Nkrumah as were all other persons or groups in the state. Perhaps they were far more thoroughly controlled; party functionaries had actually no other place to go.

The same referendum authorized the President, constitutionally now, "for reasons which to him appear sufficient [to] remove from office a Judge of the Supreme Court or a Judge of the High

Court."[43] One week after the amendment had received presidential assent, Nkrumah proceeded to remove from the Supreme Court and from the High Court judges whom he deemed not in accord with his conception of justice. Another constitutional amendment made appointment of a presidential commission to conduct public inquiries a matter of presidential instead of cabinet discretion.[44]

In the same year, several statutory changes were made in an attempt to tidy up the cluttered machinery of law enforcement; others created more confusion and further undermined what remained of a bona fide legal structure.

Not content with possessing all powers needed to spirit away opponents and keep them out of circulation, incommunicado if necessary, but still finding it desirable to maintain the semblance of legality—perhaps thinking of staged political trials—Nkrumah made some further adjustments in the machinery of Nkrumaist political justice. The Special Criminal Division of the High Court, the most critical judicial organ in matters of presidential security, was reorganized to ensure complete control over proceedings and results. The presiding judge, whoever he was, was not likely to defy the hand that held the power of instant dismissal as well as the power of permanent foreclosure of any other opportunity for judicial service in Ghana. However, not taking any chances with the jurists who might try to preserve some vestige of justice, Nkrumah added a jury of twelve as a further security measure. On the face of it, this appeared to be a correction of an omission in the 1961 Criminal Procedure (Amendment) Act and an acknowledgment of the rule of the people, which was now to have commenced in earnest. In practice, membership on the jury was to be confined to loyal followers of Kwame Nkrumah, chosen from such sources as the Kwame Nkrumah Institute of Ideology at Winneba.[45]

In May, 1964, all previous Preventive Detention legislation was consolidated in the Preventive Detention Act of 1964, suggesting that this feature of Nkrumaist rule was now part of Ghana's living constitution.

The Habeas Corpus Act was passed in 1964 to retain a vestige of respectability in the eyes of the legal profession. Under it, any person alleging that he was being "unlawfully detained" could apply to the High Court or any judge for an inquiry into the cause of his detention (Section 1). Under Section 4, the High Court was to take certain actions "unless satisfied that the detention is in accordance with law." In light of the President's sweeping powers, the intricate web of security legislation, and the fact that judges could now be removed at will by the President, it was extremely unlikely that any judge would find "unlawful" the detention of a person known to have been antagonistic to the President. To cite one of many statutory safeguards against premature release of a person or unwelcome exposure of judicial error or caprice, a provision in the Presidential Affairs (Amendment) Act of 1962 stipulated that "all actions or claims against the President are actions against the Republic" and that before being filed in the appropriate court such claims "shall first be served on the Attorney General *and his fiat obtained* [italics added]."[46] The Attorney General was, of course, the President's personal choice and subject to instant dismissal on the President's fiat.

On October 1, 1964, it was ordered that the Special Branch of the Ghana police be "disintegrated" and its security function be transferred to the President's Security Service under the general heading Special Services. This action had the effect of removing from the security and detention apparatus the sole remaining element of government having professional integrity and political detachment—namely, the police. Until that moment, Special Branch—incidentally, under two of the principal leaders of the 1966 coup. J. W. K. Harlley and A. K. Deku—had shared with the presidential Security Service the responsibilities for internal security, surveillance, arrests, and detention. As part of the police service, Special Branch had nominally been under the Minister of Interior. Also transferred from the police to the Office of the President was the sensitive Border Control.[47]

IV

Building the Political Machine (II)

"In the general course of human nature," wrote Alexander Hamilton in *The Federalist* (No. 79), "a power over a man's subsistence amounts to a power over his will." The truth of this maxim has been known to rulers and has been a basis of politics since the beginning of organized society. Next to physical force directly applied, the force derived from control over the means of subsistence seems to be the most effective instrument of political persuasion.

The new leaders of Ghana, in taking over the responsibilities of government from the colonial regime, found the lion's share of the subsistence control apparatus still in non-African hands. To change this situation as rapidly as possible became a matter of highest priority. A first step toward that objective—to be specific, toward the objective of securing such control for Nkrumah—was the creation of an economic power base under the direct and immediate control of Nkrumah.

Creating a Private Base

Since time immemorial, political leaders finding themselves in possession of the keys to the treasury appear to have been unable to resist temptation. Nkrumah was no exception. Over the years, by one means or another, including extortion and acceptance of bribes, he appears to have extracted from a variety of sources

65

enough private wealth to make him a multimillionaire. Added to the amounts deposited in banks in Ghana and abroad were extensive real estate holdings and commercial property worth several million pounds.[1]

One motivation for accumulation of substantial private wealth, at home and abroad—aside from ordinary human considerations stemming from avarice and greed—related to the fear of sudden loss of power, especially during the early stages. A nest egg abroad was a form of political insurance, a strategic reserve to facilitate a return to power. The political machine also required the creation of a privately controlled economic base. Effective domination of the political control machinery, in a relatively small country, could best be achieved through manipulation of funds concealed from public view and beyond the reach of auditors.

Opportunities for self-enrichment were plentiful. They were provided by access to the accumulated reserves placed at the disposal of the incoming regime by the departing colonial administration, by the gradually increasing inflow of capital investments, and by the ever more substantial government contracts let in conjunction with the expanding development program. In due course, by Ghanaian standards enormous opportunities for graft materialized. Foreign and domestic contractors and businessmen were pressured into paying commissions or outright donations purportedly to support the CPP. The National Development Company (NADECO) had been organized to serve as a collecting agency for these funds. Through concealed accounts and complete domination of the Company's Board, Nkrumah was able to divert these funds at will into whatever channels and for whatever purposes he wanted; he clearly treated the whole enterprise as though it were his personal property. Although a substantial share of the funds thus collected was indeed paid to party officers and functionaries, the situation was such as to suggest that for CPP one had to read Nkrumah's personal political machine. The suggestion in Nkrumah's will, prepared shortly before his fall, that NADECO had been created to serve as the main financial support of the party after his death cannot be taken seriously. Throughout his career, he failed to make adequate provision for the survival of the party, let alone for its operation.

To secure personal control over the more lucrative commissions extracted for major contracts in the multimillion-pound range, Nkrumah awarded such contracts personally without reference to the cabinet, the appropriate minister, the cabinet's contract committee, or any other agency normally associated with the granting of major contracts. This procedure also placed him in a position to receive any of the more attractive bribes competing businessmen were wont to offer.[2]

Whatever the rationale for Nkrumah's private transactions, it had long been clear that presidential spending could not be explained solely by public appropriations. Whether as custodian of party funds or capitalist on his own account, Nkrumah appears to have been in command of independent resources of considerable magnitude.

In a small country, the political leverage derived from private wealth is considerable, probably proportionately greater than in a larger country. And Nkrumah had other leverage at his disposal—namely, public funds.

Subsistence Control: Through Public Funds

As soon as it became feasible, Nkrumah brought the entire development program under his direct personal supervision and control. Establishing a special office for that purpose at his headquarters, he assumed direct personal command over spending of the development funds, exceeding £6 million in 1964–65.

Before attributing Machiavellian motives to Nkrumah, it must be acknowledged, in all fairness, that the administrative structure that he inherited from the colonial regime was not conditioned to operate decisively and promptly. Urgent key projects, such as the development of the Volta River hydroelectric-power potential had to be transferred from the slow-moving, red-tape–addicted civil service. Placing over-all control of this vital segment of Ghana's governmental machinery in his own hands was entirely unobjectionable and in keeping with sound administrative and political practice.

However, it would require an extraordinarily short-sighted person not to see that in the absence of adequate accounting and control machinery sufficiently independent to subject the Prime Minister's office to close scrutiny and, if necessary, to public exposure, the fortunes of the personal political machine could be enhanced enormously through certain administrative changes.

The public funds within Nkrumah's sphere of influence under the development rubric constituted by far the largest of all annual expenditures. The first Development Plan, launched in 1952 and expected to run through 1957, envisaged expenditures of up to £74 million. By 1955, £50 million had been spent.[3] While substantial sums were applied to socially worth-while projects under carefully controlled conditions, equally substantial sums were used to strengthen Nkrumah's power and build the political machine.

Between 1955 and 1956, the actual expenditures controlled by the Prime Minister and paid out of the consolidated fund increased from 2 per cent to 30 per cent of the total. Once Nkrumah had extended his power over the rest of the government, the percentage nominally under the Prime Minister, or President, decreased; but at that point it no longer mattered.[4]

The first scandal broke in 1953 with allegations of bribery and corruption against one cabinet minister, who was forced to resign.[5] However, the Commission of Enquiry, in response to charges by the Parliamentary opposition of cabinet (i.e., Nkrumah) complicity, found that "allegations of general misconduct among those holding high office in the Gold Coast were not substantiated."[6] Three years later, in 1956, the Jibowu Commission investigating allegations that public funds belonging to the Cocoa Purchasing Company had been misappropriated for "political purposes," with an eye to the 1953 whitewash, found that "most of the irregularities which we have had to investigate would have been prevented if the Government had taken a firm stand to check and punish irregularities of the type complained about . . . as far back as 1953."

None of the numerous writers evaluating the Jibowu Commission's findings saw through the assertion in the Commission's report that the Cocoa Purchasing Company had been "controlled by the Convention People's Party" and that the misused funds had been applied "for the purpose of winning adherents for the CPP" by giving loans mainly to "party sympathizers."[7] The habitual acceptance of labels, no matter how inapplicable, still prevailed. One spoke of the party when one should have spoken of the personal political machine growing within and even outside the party, with the powerful assistance of public funds dispensed under the direction of a political boss.

By 1960, no person in Ghana would dare suggest out loud that Nkrumah might have used public funds for purposes other than those prescribed by statute and regulation. Parliament, and its Public Accounts Committee, while diligently digging around in various peripheral sectors of government and administration, meticulously avoided the central presidential preserves. Since the President's powers and responsibilities extended rather far afield, the diggings were confined to petty theft and mismanagement of modest public funds. The Public Accounts Committee's detection devices were most delicately attuned to avoid setting off political dynamite. Needless to say, the "fearless" Ghanaian press knew better than to raise questions concerning the Office of the President.

How did Nkrumah employ the private wealth and the public funds at his disposal to further his political objectives? After the coup, Lieutenant General J. A. Ankrah succinctly summarized the situation: "We believe that some of Nkrumah's followers joined the disbanded Convention People's Party in order to get their daily bread, of which Kwame Nkrumah had cunningly maneuvered himself into being the largest donor in the country."[8] He should have included the political machine as the principal beneficiary.

Through the Deputy Secretary to the Cabinet, T. K. Impraim,

W. M. Q. Halm of the Bank of Ghana, or his financial adviser, E. Ayeh-Kumi, Nkrumah operated a privately controlled personal loan service (sometimes no interest was charged) through which he rewarded personal and political supporters and friends. Loans were frequently drawn from the Contingency Fund, from any number of private bank accounts at home and abroad, and from a variety of Government-owned or controlled corporations. The Housing Corporation was used by Nkrumah to allocate houses to loyal supporters, key persons in the several auxiliary organizations which were feeding the political machine. Jobs were allocated or denied, lucrative trading opportunities opened or closed, and lush contracts were thrown in the direction of the more loyal supporters. The technique was perhaps most clearly revealed in an incident brought to light after the coup.

T. D. Baffoe, then Editor of the *Ghanaian Times*, was called, in 1962, to appear before Nkrumah because of an editorial he had written which had caused Nkrumah "some embarrassment." Apparently, Baffoe had drawn Nkrumah's displeasure on other occasions, and had been dismissed from a post earlier. Baffoe's account of what transpired at the interview illuminates Nkrumah's technique: "After a good brushing from the ex-President, [Nkrumah] in a manner typical of him, at the time wanted to reduce tensions. So he asked Adamafio, who was present, to contact T. K. Impraim and see if he could get me one of the houses built for the Ministry of Health which were lying vacant at the time." Additional evidence brought out at that time before the Effah Commission revealed that identical methods were employed by Nkrumah to bribe all editors of the three major Nkrumaist papers.[9]

Aware that numerous ministers and other leaders knew of his financial manipulations, he allowed them, in the tradition of all political-machine bosses, to engage in similar practices, in some instances even encouraging them, or he invited them to become his accomplices, only to use his knowledge of their transgressions to his own purposes.[10] He compelled many to keep silent about his own activities, and generally to accept one-man rule, the bypassing of the cabinet and the party Central Committee, the unconstitutional conduct of government, and so on.

Those most vulnerable to pressure derived from control over means of subsistence were the traditional chiefs. Under a variety of legislative acts, but also in accordance with a tradition going back to colonial days, they were very much dependent upon executive approval, which in this case meant approval from the political machine. The cold political reality was that at no time did they pose a substantive security threat to Nkrumah. To be on the safe side, however, the regime employed its entire arsenal, statutory and straight political pressure, to secure their cooperation.[11]

One particularly useful formula for the construction of a personal political machine has been that of the democratic welfare state or the related socialist state. Throughout the world, under banners of "public welfare," "socialist construction," "anticapitalism," and, as of late, "antineocolonialism," attempts are made to persuade the public that whatever is done with the national wealth must of necessity be for the public good if it is done in the people's name.

It stands to reason that it occurred to Nkrumah that whereas a modest political machine can be built in a relatively free and open society, a much larger and all-inclusive political machine can be built more successfully in the socialist state, where public and private domains are merged into one.

PERSONNEL AND GROUP MANAGEMENT

The "People"

"Plato's description," writes a contemporary student of political development, "of the means by which the despot appeals to the people, isolates and eliminates his enemies, and builds up his personal strength is a far less misleading guide to what has taken place in Ghana and other new states than many things written yesterday."[12] Underlying this comment and much of social-science analysis today is an assumption, not necessarily valid, that the "people" in a country like Ghana possess sufficient intrinsic social cohesion to make an appeal to them politically meaningful. Yet anyone who has witnessed the Ghanaian "people" march on an embassy, a library, or a university, or engage in some similar revolutionary pursuit cannot fail to harbor considerable skepticism concerning the validity of the assumption.

What of the thesis that Nkrumah seized and maintained power by skillful manipulation of diverse competing groups and organizations? That he utilized the support of various groups in his march to power is beyond doubt. In the beginning, there were the Standard VI (primary-school graduates) "boys," the nucleus of his early political organization. If ever there was a group utterly dependent on a leader and wholly incapable of seizing, let alone maintaining, power by itself, it was that group. There were the veterans of World War II, the real core of the 1948 demonstration that sparked the riots that in turn sparked what became known as the Gold Coast Revolution. This group faded into the background, and into political limbo, as suddenly as it had emerged.

The group probably most influential in the sector of mass communications—i.e., the "grapevine"—and therefore most instrumental in Nkrumah's rise to power was the women engaged in trade, commerce, and marketing. Strategically situated in the retail trade, food distribution, transport—they were the owners of the "mammy wagons"—these women dominated the major communication arteries in the country, spreading their influence along the country's supply and distribution routes. Nkrumah assiduously cultivated that source of support throughout his political career.

Although nominally organized in the National Council of Ghana Women, under the CPP Constitution, an "integral wing of the party," the trading women remained a fiercely independent lot, trading their support of Nkrumah for material benefits. When these benefits dried up, as a result of the deteriorating economic situation and resultant shortages, restrictions, and persecutions of petty traders, the support waned. Insistence by the regime on nationalization of trade most probably fed the flames of hostility. Knowledge of widespread corruption and favoritism among the government officials probably strengthened the trading women's determination to demand their fair share.

As his ability to dispense material benefits to the group as a whole dwindled, Nkrumah resorted to bribery of key leaders. It is most unlikely, however, that he feared this particular group as a potent political force. Aside from occasional noisy demonstrations, the political edge of organized womenhood was easily dulled. Personal loans, gifts, free houses, choice appointments to sinecures for the leaders plus spot concessions to their followers in the form of tax relief, and sporadic relaxation of certain import restrictions, as well as spectacular "investigations" into their grievances, took care of that problem.[13]

The traditional rulers, another key element in the formation of what might be termed public opinion in Ghana, also were bribed, or threatened, into submission. In addition to the aforementioned subsistence control, Nkrumah was able to exercise control over recalcitrant chiefs through a whole arsenal of devices. Exploiting intratribal rivalries to the fullest, he had most chiefs practically eating out of his hand. Through a special section in the Office of the President, he manipulated the chiefs, and through them, the traditional councils, like so many puppets. There was not a council whose affairs could stand scrutiny by a government auditor; there were exceedingly few chiefs who had not, at one time or another, run into conflict with the law and who, therefore, feared exposure; unlike protected party leaders, the chiefs felt constantly the hot breath of rival claimants. Under the circumstances, traditional rulers became most helpful props of Nkrumah's political machine. Those who would not cooperate, and were not amenable to bribery, were simply banished into the political and economic wilderness.

Then there were the Ghanaian wholesale traders—the shipping tycoons, timber merchants, cocoa dealers, transport owners, textile importers, and food distributors—who had assisted in the disturbances of 1948. Their grievances, roughly approximating those of the North American traders who rebelled against British rule in 1776, were not politically organized, had no distinct political goals, and faded away as a political force. There remained the party, the trade unions, the armed forces, and the civil service.

The Party

By a curious process of reasoning, many observers of the Ghanaian political scene have concluded that there existed in Ghana, from the beginning (i.e., from 1949 onward), a mass movement or an organization that was engaged in some form of mass mobilization. To this observer, after ten years of intermittent study of the Ghanaian political scene, such a conclusion rests on an illusion compounded of wishful thinking, unresearched hypotheses, and purposeful political propaganda.[14] It is a case of mistaking appearance for substance. There is no reliable evidence at all that the Convention People's Party as a party has ever been capable of, or has engaged in, what might justifiably be termed mass-mobilization activity or that Nkrumah, its builder, ever actually wanted it to perform that function. He expected the party organization to help him to power and to keep him there. All that can actually be said of the party is that it succeeded, in 1951, 1954, and 1956, in *contributing* to the capture of majorities in the several legislatures. But that is a far cry from mass mobilization.

In Ghana, where the preconditions for mass organization were difficult to create, it was one thing to coax, cajole, trick, and lead 5 to 15 per cent of the total adult population to the polls and persuade them to cast their ballots into the box featuring the red cockerel, the emblem of the CPP; it was quite another to claim that these people, by casting little colored slips of paper into ballot boxes, had become integral parts of a mass organization, had been ideologically or otherwise mobilized, shared in any meaningful way the political objectives of the party, and could be relied upon to support other tasks set for them by the party leadership. As a matter of fact, traditional chiefs, who had opted for the CPP in the three elections of 1951, 1954, and 1956, may deserve a far greater share of the credit than the party for the party's impressive victories at the polls. In the urban centers, market women helped mightily, probably providing the major assist.[15]

To be sure, Nkrumah repeatedly assigned to the party what might be described as mass-mobilization functions. Also, numerous efforts were made to set up—as distinct from operate—an impressive number of party auxiliaries, which were expected, in theory, to back up Nkrumah's program in every section of the country.

The party press and individual leaders on the hustings expended much energy exhorting the public to rally to the support of the socialist construction program, to the support of Osagyefo, the Leader, to the defense of the revolution, to defeat black-marketing, corruption, "neocolonialist subversion," administrative negligence. What is of signal importance is that there is little if any concrete evidence that these exhortations ever were acted upon, that they ever were *in fact* translated into action toward the ends held up as desirable. There is evidence, however, in the President's own speeches and in occasional references in Parliament, that the opposite was the case —i.e., that mass-mobilization was not getting under way.

There were several reasons for this. First, Ghanaian society lacked the infrastructure required for effective mobilization of large and relatively undeveloped human resources. Ghana also lacked an ideology that could be used to mobilize the masses. Most important in the context of this study is the probability that *effective* mass mobilization would have run counter to Nkrumah's interests. Intent on securing power for himself, Nkrumah could not favor mass action of any kind. Rival centers of power and rival political machines inevitably would form. Mass action often gets out of control. It is therefore doubtful that Nkrumah was interested in the mass-mobilization state except to the extent that mass mobilization could be harnessed securely to the political machine, and that could not be done reliably.

As has been pointed out, a major share of the illicit funds acquired by Nkrumah was alleged to have been earmarked for the party. A good deal, of course, did reach the party. What is materially important for our purposes, however, is that Nkrumah was the party: he controlled the Central Committee and the functionaries all the way down. Whatever funds eventually reached the party were not applied to mass mobilization. The funds were used for purposes related to the personal machine. Decisions concerning their disposition were made in the name of the party by the simple expedient of Nkrumah's informing an *ad hoc* gathering of a set of Central Committee members of his decision on one matter, and at another time using another set for ratification of another decision.

The Trade Union Movement

As in a number of other countries adopting totalitarian measures after independence, the trade unions were quickly brought to heel and directed to address themselves to the new tasks of national construction. That was reasonable enough. Accordingly, an Industrial Relations Act was passed in 1958 to consolidate the unions and to integrate them with the CPP. After that, the unions were expected to concentrate on political tasks set by the new supreme employer, the state. But some of the functionaries—especially the Secretary General of the Trade Union Congress (TUC), John Tettegah—saw the writing on the wall and protested. Tettegah insisted on organizational independence, but to no avail. He was removed and during the two years of his absence, in the comic-opera Workers Brigade, the TUC was securely tied, not to the party—which did not really exist—but to the personal political machine.[16] When Tettegah returned to the TUC he found himself encircled by Nkrumah's personal appointees and agents.

To the observer easily impressed by figures, the Ghanaian TUC indeed appeared to be a mass movement. In February, 1961, a suspicious and not very sophisticated CPP Member of Parliament, believing he had caught a glimpse of a counterrevolutionary movement, complained:

It seems to me that the Trade Union Congress is being organized to such an extent that the party which is in power is losing its identity. I say this because from the various documents available in this country we have seen that one union alone has been able to register about 275,000 members. If we compare this membership of one union of the TUC to the total population of Ghana—which is seven million—we can clearly see that in future we shall have a "labour" Government instead of a CPP Government.[17]

The response from John Tettegah was revealing, albeit somewhat clouded by wishful thinking. With the savage edge of a totalitarian-minded labor boss, he assured the "workers" that "the Osagyefo and the Party have the appropriate machinery to deal with him"—i.e., with the indiscreet MP.[18] Had he omitted "the Party," he would have been more correct. Tettegah, on showing signs of succumbing to temptations of a political nature, was once more removed from his position, and a new Secretary General, more loyal to the Leader, was installed in his place.

Realistically, in terms of inner organizational strength, revolutionary *élan*, and financial means, neither the trade unions nor the party, acting alone or together, could have been expected to engineer a successful coup against personal rule. Certainly the Security Service and Nkrumah's unofficial personal informers enabled him to detect and foil any substantive move from these quarters to unseat him. After the coup, it was revealed that the new Secretary General, Kwaw Ampah, had been supplied by Nkrumah with a slush fund to bribe lesser functionaries and recruit them for the political machine.

Even where trade union demands were advanced on justifiable, purely economic grounds, Nkrumah was adequately equipped to resist such pressure. The abortive strikes of 1961, started significantly while the leader was abroad, demonstrated that workers, no matter how justified their grievances, could not hope to succeed in pressing their demands without assistance from the army or police.

The Armed Forces and the Police

To minimize the chances of an armed forces–initiated or supported counterrevolution, Nkrumah took a number of special steps. From the earliest opportunity, he reserved the defense portfolio to himself, exercising personal and direct supervision over the selection and promotion of officers, supervision of postings, control over appropriations, expenditures, and supplies. The creation of a Ministry of Defense did not change the control structure in the least.

Through careful balancing of the several divergent tribal elements within the armed forces and through the development of channels of communication and informer services that permitted any loyalist to circumvent superior officers and the minister and contact the Commander-in-Chief directly, Nkrumah welded the armed forces to the personal political machine. Following the advice given by Soviet experts he allowed the Security Service to infiltrate the armed forces.

In view of the unreliability of the so-called revolutionary mass organizations, Nkrumah had for a long time regarded the armed forces, primarily the army, next to the Security Service, as the principal support of the political machine—not only against external threats, whatever those might have been, but also against internal threats. In time, again under advice from Eastern specialists in revolutionary security, he concluded that the Sandhurst-trained officers corps could not be trusted. In 1960, as a first step to improve the revolutionary dedication of the army, and especially of the contingents seconded to serve as his bodyguard, he accepted an invitation to send 400 candidates to the Soviet Union for officer training; he did this over the objections of senior army officers.[19] In time, he was to realize that this may well have set off the reaction among older officers that led eventually to his overthrow.

The attempt on his life of January 2, 1964, caused him to revise once again his estimate of the reliability of the police, partly because the alleged perpetrator of the attempt had been a member of the police force or because evidence, genuine or contrived, pointed to complicity or laxity on the part of high police officers. The resulting purge of the police command, which brought J. W. K. Harlley to the top position and the reassignment of the presidential guard function to army units, reflected one of the special problems of personal rule: how to protect the ruler, secure the personal political machine, and yet prevent the protecting forces from gaining too much power.

Nkrumah's answer to that vexing problem was the creation of a special force, or private army, modeled after Hitler's notorious SS. Unfortunately for Nkrumah, he found few soldiers in Ghana to train such a force and had to rely again on foreign instructors, from the East in this case. This compounded his problem, for the employment of foreigners, especially for what regular officers regarded as subversive activities, ran counter to the high-priority Africanization program that had resulted in the removal of British officers from Ghana. Moreover, the Hitler —or was it the Stalin?—model was irrelevant because unlike his Nazi or Communist counterparts, Nkrumah lacked the indigenous material required for the ruthless and efficient instruments of suppression represented by the SS and the NKVD. He also lacked a cause around which to rally a fanatically loyal protective force.

Personal Relations and Friendships

One essential ingredient in the management of power is the management of individuals.

Nkrumah's friends were mainly non-Ghanaians. He used Ghanaians but did not value them as friends. What might have appeared as friendship invariably turned into disinterest at best, enmity at worst. Of his early collaborators—Ashie Nikoe, William Ofori Atta, Joe Appiah, Awooner Renner, Kurankyi-Taylor, and Nancy Tsiboe—only the last-named had returned to the circle when the end came; even she had joined the mass defection from Nkrumah in 1954 and had revealed, in public attacks on him, intense personal disappointment, if not hatred. Joe Appiah, at one time his personal representative in London, broke with him in 1954, never to resume the friendship. Komla Gbedemah, who kept the embryonic machine going while Nkrumah languished in prison from 1950 to 1951, was cut down politically and forced to go into exile to save himself. Ako Adjei, who had first brought the young Nkrumah to the attention of the nationalist leader-ship in the Gold Coast, barely escaped execution after being destroyed politically. Kojo Botsio and Kofi Baako were suspect and were kept on the political periphery. Nana Kobina Nketsia, iv, another member of the group of pre-independence political "prison graduates," failed in his strenuous efforts to reassure Nkrumah of his reliability and was dropped.

Nkrumah's suspicion of, or aversion to, more intelligent and free-ranging minds created an insurmountable barrier between himself and the Ghanaian intelligentsia. His hostility toward that group which he rationalized as due to their lack of popu-larity with, and sensitivity to, the needs of the masses—was ex-acerbated by the barely concealed disdain of the Ghanaian social elite, who considered Nkrumah a relative upstart.

Nkrumah tolerated intelligence only in those who were wholly subservient or totally apolitical, and, in the main, only if they were foreign citizens. Herein lies the explanation for the predominance of foreigners among his closer collaborators, such as Bing, Hodgkin, Basner, Bellamy, Nunn May, and Hanna Reitsch. These people recommended themselves because of their utter lack of interest in Ghanaian political affairs. Their main interests being outside the country, they posed no threat to Kwame Nkrumah. Most wanted something from him—a base of operations, security, asylum, prestige. Even his longtime private secretary, Erica Powell, became *persona non grata* when she dared to concern herself independently with controversial matters in Ghana.

Nkrumah relied heavily on the weaknesses and frailties of his collaborators in keeping them in line. At the top levels of leadership, in the cabinet, the party Central Committee, the trade unions, the various state enterprises, the farmers' organizations, and the courts, he exploited on greed, vanity, and ambition to the fullest.[20] His success is evidenced by the fact that resignations from office were rare. In spite of abusive, humiliating, and insulting treatment, only one cabinet member resigned voluntarily; that was the proud and dignified veteran nationalist Archie Casely Hayford. None of the other cabinet members, though some protested discreetly, resigned over corruption, mismanagement, subversion of the constitution, or poor economic and fiscal planning. All wanted the perquisites of office, shrewdly allocated and manipulated by Nkrumah.[21]

Distrust of the personal motivations of the people around him apparently caused him to use Security Service, private informers, and the aforementioned "holy man" to secure for himself a degree of psychological control over his associates.[22] During his final years in office, his desire to be informed on all relationships and social and political crosscurrents that were remotely relevant to his expanded sphere of interest became an obsession.

Much has been made of Nkrumah's preference for Nzimas,

members of his own tribe. Nzimas certainly predominated among his closest advisers, confidants, and collaborators, particularly among security officers; E. Ayeh-Kumi and the Yankey father and son team were among the better known. Pending further study, I am of the opinion that this preference was mainly, if not exclusively, a personal security measure. It is most unlikely that it had any significant bearing on Nkrumah's political philosophy or style of rule.

IDEOLOGY, IDEOLOGISTS, AND THE PERSONALITY CULT

Under certain conditions, ideology can undoubtedly contribute to the achievement of social and economic goals, but in Nkrumah's Ghana a suitable ideology had not been developed; conditions were not favorable to either the development of an ideology or to its application.

Communication alone posed a serious problem, although it has been commonly ignored by observers. Not only was the level of education low (20 per cent literacy), but the official language of government and administration, English, was not the mother tongue of the population. Assuming that Nkrumah actually intended to communicate his ideas, policy proposals, values, and ideological propositions to the public at large, and assuming that the public's participation was required for the fulfillment of certain administrative, social, and ideological goals, it was extremely probable that such participation would be quite desultory, confused, and multidirectional. Fortunately for Nkrumah, widespread public comprehension of his ideological proposals and widespread public participation—aside from ceremonial participation—were not required to implement his *real* objectives, as against the cover objectives that from time to time were held up for public inspection and discussion in election campaigns, the party press, and political oratory.

Realistically or not, genuinely or fraudulently, Nkrumah certainly seemed to devote an extraordinarily large share of his time and a considerable share of his country's scarce manpower and material resources to what might be called ideological pursuits. From his college days to the end of his rule, he personally encouraged and directed political planning and discussion groups, reading circles, councils, committees, task forces, all to provide guidance and impetus to his revolutionary program. Sections of the personal political machine were detached and directed to busy themselves with developing political strategies for transforming Ghana into a socialist society.

The most important of the groups formed on Nkrumah's initiative—invariably composed of politically impotent individuals—were the League of Ghana Patriots, the National Association of Socialist Students' Organizations (NASSO), and the Party Vanguard Activists (PVA).[23]

Just as some observers have attributed political, organizational, and other capabilities to the CPP that it demonstrably did not possess, the young, inexperienced, intellectually untrained, and often wild-eyed "ideologists" among Kwame Nkrumah's followers have been credited with nonexistent skills and capabilities, including the ability to generate political power and influence.

Where a number of highly motivated ideologists are found, even if motivation is shallow and ideology a patchwork of borrowed, undigested, socially irrelevant propositions, it is often generalized that political influence must result. This appears to be based on the assumption that where there is a will to influence, the capability to influence must follow. But power and influence do not flow from will alone.

"Left" versus "Right"

We are told, for example, that "the vanguardist groups constitute the mechanism whereby Nkrumah hopes to be able to move the Ghanaian—and the African—masses toward an economic revolution."[24] Accepting this highly inappropriate concept of a "mechanism," some observers then ascribe to these little groups great potentialities within the power constellation swirling around the President. According to that view, the President played these groups—collectively and misleadingly referred to as "the Left"—against what is equally misleadingly termed "the Right." All this to serve his own ends.[25]

In a purely peripheral, palace-intrigue sense, he may well have engaged in certain maneuvers, at one time favoring elements on the Left, at another time shifting his favors to elements on the Right; but never did he seem to favor an entire section of the political spectrum.

The most crucial aspect of the problem is consistently left out in speculations concerning the role of the ideologists in creating and operating the political machine—namely, their utter lack of qualifications for high-level politics, political organizations, mass mobilization, and policy determination.

What did the Left in Ghana really represent? There is no evidence that those who generalize on the subject have made any real effort to take a close look. The social and political setting alone militated against creation of an effective corps to sustain a revolutionary spearhead, or "vanguard." One-man rule and the effects of the political machine combined to dissipate whatever revolutionary *élan* there may have been among the young students who gathered around Nkrumah in the 1940's and 1950's. As in the United States during the McCarthy period, the years of persecution, arbitrary interference, and thought control produced a situation where only cautious mediocrities rose to the top (along with a sprinkling of genuine supporters of Nkrumah).

One-man rule meant that persons intellectually superior to the ruler must be excluded from the inner councils; thus advancement went to intellectual mediocrity rather than intelligence, to abject submission rather than independence of thought. At the top, it produced an air of cynicism and intellectual anemia. At the lower levels, it created confusion, irresolution, phrase-mongering, and unmitigated opportunism. The foregoing assessment of the people around him was periodically made by Nkrumah himself, although he could not admit the root cause of the situation.[26]

Even if capable of independent political action and intent on undertaking it, NASSO, PVA, the informal association of graduates of the Winneba Ideological Institute, the Nkrumaist forums, and other similarly oriented groups would have found the setting extremely unfavorable; the effects of the divide-and-rule technique would quickly have become apparent to would-be plotters. It would soon have been discovered that all accessible, important channels of communication, required for swift and effective action, were in the secure control of the political machine.[27]

To characterize the Ghanaian Left as powerful or potentially so, as cohesive, maneuverable, operationally meaningful, and capable, was to ignore the administrative jungle that Nkrumah had created and that opposition groups would have had to master if they were to take effective action through political channels. To evaluate the Left as capable of extracting concessions from Nkrumah in return for their support was to ignore Nkrumah's demonstrated political acumen and watchfulness. It is hard to imagine a weaker group, a group more dependent on one leader for its very survival than the vaunted Ghanaian Left.

What members of the Left had been able to do, and with reasonable success, was to provide Nkrumah with sets of rationales—literally so in *Consciencism*[28]—that he could use to cloak the old-fashioned, garden-variety political machine in ideologically respectable garments. They also provided his vague formulations of Africa's problems with sets of seemingly concrete action programs—e.g., "union government," continental economic union, and liberation of the remaining holds of "imperialism." Deprived of access to the effective centers of power, which were well scattered throughout the state and society, they were sharply set back when too ambitious and were confined in the main to spheres of political ritual and propaganda. No matter how shrilly or insistently they sought to prescribe rules of conduct for officials, develop rules of behavior for the masses, in editorials, speeches, and memoranda to the Leader, they were never more than appendages to power in the manner of court philosophers of old. Their energies were devoted to building ideological castles in the sands of time.[29]

As for substantive political action, examples like the death sentences (later commuted to life imprisonment) of party stalwarts like Ako Adjei, Tawia Adamafio, and H. H. Cofie-Crabbe were meant to drive home a basic point that was not likely to be lost on actual or potential anti-Nkrumah conspirators within the Left. If the Leader commanded "turn left," one followed. If he commanded the opposite, one followed also. For whatever Nkrumah wanted was, by definition, correct ideology. It was Nkrumaism.

Nkrumaism: An Instrument of the Machine

Generally, ideology is regarded as related only to state and society. It is descriptive of beliefs regarding facts and values related to the way society is and ought to be organized, to the ends that are to be attained, the purposes and functions of social institutions and processes. However, as one writer puts it: "The word 'ideology' is sometimes applied to almost any set of beliefs about what ought to be, provided they are reasonably coherent and consistent."[30] This applies in particular to the aggregate of writings collectively known as "African socialism."

Perhaps because of the novelty of encountering what appears to be ideological activity in formerly colonial Africa, or perhaps because "socialism" *appears* to be an eminently suitable framework for the rapid, even forced, solution of the developmental problems confronting the newly independent states, writers on the subject tend to be singularly uncritical toward such ideological formulations. Very little attention, for example, has been paid to social relevance. Nkrumaism has been a prime beneficiary of this tendency.[31]

As one experienced student of Ghanaian affairs saw it: "If the *philosophy* of Nkrumaism is by no means organized and program-matic, it is *clearly a language* of socialism, progress, and development [italics added].''[32] But language, as students of communication science are aware, conceals as much as it reveals. The language of Nkrumaism was no exception. In addition to having value to state and society, to social "progress and development"— depending on one's point of view, or ideology—the language had instrumental value in the building and operation of the political machine, a process related to what social scientists know as "symbol manipulation." In Nkrumaist Ghana, language was used as a device to herd substantial segments of the population into intellectual enclosures with boundaries determined by the personal ruler's strategy and tactics. This was possible because as a "language" it was vague enough to mean anything—anything at all.

Nkrumah set the pace, selected the means and the methods, delineated the areas within which "ideology" was to apply, and dictated what was to be translated into practice and what was not. He controlled the sluice gates separating word from deed, theory from practice. In the main, Nkrumaism was a verbalization of the requirements of the personal political machine. Professional scribes and amateurs, along with the Ghanaian Left, were set to the task of providing the coherence and internal consistency required to give a semblance of philosophy to the chaotic assemblage of ideas and fantasies borrowed from all parts of the world and from all periods of history, frequently out of context.

Personality Cult

The dividing line between the canons of religion and those of an ideology is at times difficult to locate. This is partly because either term can be used carelessly, partly because both share certain elements, particularly symbols; also both can be charged with emotion, and permeated with transcendental, metaphysical notions. Under Nkrumaist rule, the so-called ideology of Nkrumaism blended into a religious phenomenon that ascribed divine characteristics to Nkrumah. The likelihood that very few people gave more than lip service to either the ideology or the religion is another matter. Personal rule certainly sought to utilize both approaches.

It all began innocently enough. Crowds made up of admirers, mostly youngsters and market women, upon seeing the young Nkrumah in the early stages of his career, would shout with pride, "Show Boy!" Soon the young leader was carried into arenas where the CPP rallied, ensconced on a chiefly throne under a resplendent umbrella, symbol of traditional rule. Few people could object. The new Africa required new leadership, and what would be more sensible than to blend the new with the old, transferring thereby the prestige and dignity of traditional office to the new leader in the interest of nation-building and modernization, a symbol of the new Africa. In due course, he assumed chiefly titles meaningful to all major tribal units in Ghana: Osagyefo, Katamanto, Kasapieko, Nufeno, etc.[33]

Nearly as understandable were the purely psychopolitical aspects referred to earlier: the effort to raise the personality of the Leader above the partisan battle, to protect his image, the sole symbol of newly won nationhood.[34]

Nkrumah's picture on postage stamps was reasonable enough. How, indeed, could the liberated people be assured that Ghana had become a sovereign state? But what had begun so innocently and reasonably slowly gathered momentum until it reached a climax of madness: Nkrumah's likeness on coins and banknotes, his name emblazoned in neon lights, his likeness cast in bronze, streets and squares named after him, his alleged birthplace declared sacred. Soon it was suggested that he was divine.

The references in "The Circle" were indicative of something transcending ordinary political ambition. Perhaps it was youthful exuberance or a reaction to the saturation of the African mind with Christian symbols under colonialism; or was it because missionary schools had pre-empted the educational field so that the political ritual of the early days took on the hue of religious revival meetings? Perhaps it was more than that. Nkrumah would not have been the first student of theology or seminarian to pervert the creed and its symbols to political purpose. There can be little doubt that the personality cult practiced and encouraged by him had all the markings of Christian religious ritual: the Apostle's creed, the martyrdom, the meditation in the wilderness, redemption, divine inspiration, immortality.[85]

There were other symbolisms. The tunic of a Stalin—or was it a Mao?—the studiousness of a philosopher-king, and always a return to the "Show Boy," although less and less so toward the end.

Censorship

That censorship was applied to all communications and information media in Ghana was quite apparent from 1961 on. Beginning with the economic crisis of that year and the inevitable inquiries into the sources of the difficulties, the regime evidenced increased sensitivity to all forms of criticism. Foreign correspondents found their dispatches censored, and several newsmen were deported on short notice. Foreign newspapers disappeared from public distribution centers for weeks, some permanently. Books containing criticism of Nkrumah were unavailable for the overwhelming majority throughout the country; they became increasingly rare on bookshelves in the Accra region. Toward the end of 1965, only one bookshop in Ghana had a reasonably wide selection, including a few books critical of Nkrumah and his rule. That was the bookshop at the University of Ghana. Foreign periodicals and news magazines, such as *Time,* were censored or entire issues banned.

Allowed to read only what suited the requirements of personal rule, Ghanaian readers were virtually cut off from the flow of events at home and abroad and confined to the local press. Foreign news appearing in the local press was exaggerated, substantially falsified, or invented. The general editorial policy of the party press seemed to have been to convey the impression that the world revolved around Ghana and that all the capitals of the world awaited with baited breath Nkrumah's next pronouncement or move. In part, this was related to the personality cult.

Late in 1964, Patrick Sloan obtained Nkrumah's willing ear with the suggestion that if socialism was to be brought to Ghana, the bookshops of the country—i.e., those few remaining—would have to be purged of materials critical of socialism and of Nkrumah personally. This led to the establishment of a committee of nine, in November, 1964, under the chairmanship of the head of the University of Ghana's Department of Philosophy, Professor Abraham, who a year later became the University's Pro-Vice Chancellor. According to its published terms of reference, the committee was to "work out a system to ensure the removal of all publications which do not reflect the ideology of the Party or are antagonistic to its ideals."[36]

A few days after formation of the committee had been announced, *The Ghanaian Times* editorialized that the committee had been set up "to look into the content of books in our schools, colleges, universities and libraries, to eliminate those in direct conflict with the ideology of the Party and the nation, and to ensure that these vital means of molding the thoughts of the people, young and old, are attuned to the aims of the society we are building."[37]

Even if a body of identifiable and classifiable ideological propositions had existed to provide useful criteria for the committee's guidance, it is most doubtful that an intelligent, discriminating selection could have been made. Ideologically, Nkrumaist Ghana was an overgrown jungle. In practice, all that the committee really had to guide them was the fact that the ideology of the party was Nkrumaism, and Nkrumaism was what the Leader said it was. Thus, for practical purposes, censorship meant selecting information useful to the construction and maintenance of the personal political machine.[38]

LAW

A great deal has been written about the purpose and function of law in the social-revolutionary society. Reduced to its essentials, the argument holds that law, being an instrument of power and having been employed as an instrument of class warfare and economic exploitation, must of necessity become a tool of the revolutionary regime in its effort to advance the course of history —i.e., it must become a tool of social engineering.[39] Of course, the Ghanaian legal structure, being mainly British in origin, was due to be adjusted to Ghanaian social requirements. However, partly because he recognized the possibilities for the personal machine in such a development and partly because he counted the legal profession and the courts among his enemies, Nkrumah eagerly endorsed and encouraged the move to "adjust" the legal structure to the requirements of the "socialist revolution."

Following a period of cautious exploration to meet objections from legal technicians, Nkrumah, under the banners of Africanization of law and of "socialist legality," prodded his legal advisers to engineer the conversion from British to what was to become Nkrumaist law.[40] In due course, a number of legal minds came forward to endow the operation with "scholarly" rationale, including a defense of the controversial dismissal of the Chief Justice in 1964.[41]

In their eagerness to give Nkrumah control over the judiciary and, more generally, over the entire legal structure, the political-machine philosophers, while straining to compose a respectable-sounding rationale for the 1964 constitutional amendment to permit presidential removal of judges, let slip this grossly distorted but revealing parody of United States experience:

> In the United States of America, the President has the power to "pack" the Federal Supreme Court, that is, to appoint new Judges to his liking. He also has the power to retire Judges before the stipulated retiring age. These were powers which President Franklin

Delano Roosevelt used very effectively in the mid-nineteen-thirties when he was fighting for his New Deal Programme. This is what the proposed amendment seeks to do.[42]

From 1960 on, the development of law in Ghana was, from the point of view of philosophy and theory, an exercise in futility, a form of shadow-boxing. Most work on the theory of law was suspended somewhere between the tenets of Anglo-Saxon political and social philosophy and jurisprudence and the demands of the personal political machine, much of it couched in pseudo-socialist, pseudo-scientific jargon and related to alleged practices and experiences in the socialist countries.

While legal practitioners, technicians, and scholars carried on in the British tradition, with a sprinkling of American, Soviet, and Eastern European legal experience, the sociopolitical foundations of law were being dismantled stone by stone. Meanwhile, the tentacles of the personal machine crept steadily not only into the judiciary but also into the law offices and the institutions of legal training.

The following illustrations may suffice to underline Nkrumah's personal interest, leading to direct personal intervention, in the field of legal training.

In 1958, an Act of Parliament created a General Legal Council. Its primary functions were supervision of legal training and matters concerning the legal profession and generally the upholding of standards of professional conduct. In 1963, the Council appointed Dr. J. B. Danquah—a man of eminent legal and professional qualifications but Nkrumah's number-one political enemy—as editor of the *Ghana Law Reports.* Upon learning this, Nkrumah issued a directive demanding termination of the appointment, threatening otherwise to cancel all government subsidies to the Council. The then Dean of the Faculty of Law at the University of Ghana, William B. Harvey, summarized the situation: "While the council fully recognized that under the governing law the President lacked power to issue such a directive, it saw no practical alternative to substantive compliance."[43] Subsequent events made it apparent that Nkrumah had become *de facto* Dean of the Faculty of Law. In time, he appointed what he termed Presidential Professors of Law—persons who could not be appointed to such a high rank through the regular academic procedures. He also took a direct hand in shaping the new "socialist" legal training program. All this because someone had persuaded him that the introduction of socialism to Ghana required government control of law as well as politics, of the Faculty of Law as well as the Department of Political Science at the University.[44]

Among the forces driving the entire legal machinery into one-man rule were the Ghanaian "ideologists" (all but one of whom were innocent of legal training), the advocates of Africanization, and the ubiquitous foreign advisers. Among the latter was one American lawyer, Robert Seidman, soon appointed Presidential Professor of Law, who undertook to prove, in a series of articles in *Spark,* that Nkrumaist rule was based on what he termed "socialist legality." In that effort, he was supported by the British lawyer D. N. Pritt, who sought to show that the "socialist legality" of Nkrumaist Ghana was the direct descendant of post-Stalinist Soviet legality.[45] Both arguments were eagerly welcomed by Nkrumah, whose concept of law was, simply stated, as a blunt, unadorned instrument of political coercion. Thus while the foreign experts and their Ghanaian seconds were weaving theoretical fabrics from their very imperfect material—very few, if any, of the experts had more than a nodding acquaintance with Soviet legal practice, for instance—Nkrumah and his apparatus gradually regressed into Stalinist practice, where law had been what Stalin said it was.

It should be noted here that the figure of Geoffrey Bing loomed large in all matters of law.

HIGHER EDUCATION AND RESEARCH

Although by 1960, and possibly earlier, Nkrumah possessed sufficient power to seize and control all aspects of state and society without fear of effective resistance, he opted in favor of a cautious approach to certain sectors, such as law and the courts. Circumstances surrounding higher education also indicated a need for caution and restraint. One of the major problems was staff recruitment. Because far too many of the East European and Soviet teachers and instructors were woefully deficient in the English language, continued dependence on teaching staff from English-speaking, primarily Western countries was indicated. This in turn suggested maintaining some degree of academic freedom, at least for a while.

However, the march to power could not tolerate indefinite delay. The battle had to be joined, and the fact that the University of Ghana had long been known as a citadel of anti-Nkrumaist thought and action in due course offered the excuse for the introduction of political control, *Gleichschaltung*, over higher education, too.

On February 24, 1963, Nkrumah—as Chancellor of the University of Ghana—turned to that problem. In the course of his address to a University audience, he touched upon the subject of academic freedom:

Teachers must be free to teach their subjects without any other concern than to convey to their students the truth as faithfully as they know it. Scholars must be free to pursue the truth and to publish the results of their researches without fear, for true scholarship fears nothing.

We know that academic freedom can be perverted and even abused. It can also become a dangerous cloak for activities outside the academic interests and pre-occupations of the community or of the university.

When I accepted the office of Chancellor, I promised you that I would do everything in my power to assist in promoting the successful development and prosperity of the University. I would like to take this opportunity to repeat this promise, and to assure you that you will have my support in all your *legitimate* endeavours in the interest of the University and the people of Ghana. [Italics added.][46]

The true meaning of what Nkrumah meant by "legitimate endeavours" became apparent without delay.

Shortly after that address, he used his presidential powers to integrate the University of Ghana and higher education and research in general with the personal political machine. Behind a façade of impressive-sounding but financially neglected "academies," committees, and commissions, control over teaching and research was transferred to the President's Office, the rationale being that these sectors were critical in the framework of national development and so presidential supervision was mandatory. As for social-science research into contemporary or future problems, presidential control meant stagnation. There were, of course, few subjects of contemporary social, economic, or political significance that would not, upon thorough investigation, expose the raw nerve of machine politics. To expect Nkrumah to authorize use of funds to facilitate such exposure would have been asking too much.[47]

In 1963 and 1964, Nkrumah increased pressure on the University of Ghana to allow him, as Chancellor, to direct certain phases of its instructional program and personnel policy. As usual, the pressure was applied with references to the need for Africanization. Under the impact of the January 2, 1964, attempt on his life—but not necessarily related to that event—Nkrumah further clarified his intent to alter the statutory relationship between the University of Ghana and the government. Although Nkrumah had been confirmed as head of the University by statute, the University of Ghana Act of 1961 had provided the framework for administrative autonomy for the University authorities. Under the statute, "the supreme governing body of the University [was to be] the University Council." On January 27,

1964, Nkrumah sent the University a letter containing six directives, all but one clearly within the jurisdiction of the statutory bodies of the University, and several actually reaching down into teaching departments, over the heads of departmental chairmen. Within a week, a mob was dispatched to impress faculty and students with the power of the President, six senior staff members were deported on a variety of grounds (two others having been arrested a short time before), and hints were broadcast from the substantial number of presidentially controlled agencies concerned with staffing, funding, and scholarships that nothing short of surrender would open the cornucopia of presidential favor to faculty, students, and officials. In this campaign, the newspapers played their assigned role, *The Ghanaian Times* commencing a weekly feature devoted to attacks on the University of Ghana and higher education in general.[48]

When the dust of this latest assault had settled, Nkrumah's control extended directly to the universities. Any professor or lecturer wishing to act as if the university still were free and autonomous, could do so at his peril. He certainly could not expect to partake of the riches so readily dispensed by the President to his favorites. A few did manage to enjoy the best of both worlds, though.

The President now enjoyed direct and indirect personal control over the purse-strings regulating salaries, promotions, new appointments, housing, equipment, and especially graduate-training facilities, the latter through research grants and scholarships. He could veto appointments of heads of faculties and departments. He controlled opportunities for travel abroad. By April, 1965, it had been demonstrated that he not only possessed the power to reach into the universities over the heads of the administrative authorities but that he was prepared to use that power whenever he saw fit.

As everywhere else, here, too, the criterion for selection by the political machine was not party membership per se but a high degree of loyalty to Nkrumah personally.

ADMINISTRATION

A Separate Branch of Government: Flagstaff House

In the Western countries, government is said to consist of three branches: executive, legislative, and judiciary. In the Communist countries, a fourth branch must be added—the Party Secretariat. In Nkrumaist Ghana, contrary to the impression conveyed in a number of scholarly discussions, the fourth branch was not the CPP but the President's Office. It combined executive, legislative, and judicial functions.

There had been many reasons for physically separating the administrative headquarters of a personal political machine from the regular, established governmental office complex. Foremost was the need for secrecy in the construction of the personal political machine. Furthermore, Nkrumah, considering himself at war with the "imperialist" states, feared their skillful and extensive intelligence operations; since he himself was deeply engaged in covert operations at home and abroad, he was not prepared to trust the senior civil servants or willing to rely on the established channels of communication. Thus he had little choice but to locate a separate center for his personal political management.[49] Such were the origins of Flagstaff House.

There, government and administration in Ghana were centered, and there, all phases of public policy and policy execution were gathered in the hands of a relatively small number of hand-picked, politically reliable civil servants acting in the President's name, under the direction of the President's secretary, who was euphemistically called Secretary to the Cabinet. Where possible, as mentioned earlier, Nkrumah selected for his inner administrative and security staff persons of Nzima origin.

The offices and agencies grouped around the official cabinet were, in terms of eminence, decision-making latitude, and political weight, mere antechambers to the President's office. The cabinet ministers were no more than highly paid messengers who drove beflagged automobiles to and from the President's Office, carried orders, made inquiries, and sought to resolve impasses stemming from the ambiguities surrounding their own positions and the apparatus of government in general.

As Flagstaff House expanded, the regular ministries lapsed into a state of subordination incompatible with the requirements of the form of government for which they had been created. Instead of the maxims of sound public administration developed in textbooks and administration manuals, the maxims of personal-machine politics dominated considerations of organization and methods, allocation of functions, and design of machinery to resolve administrative conflicts, minimize duplication, and curb expenditures. The magic formula for resolving jurisdictional conflicts and in general for all administrative considerations was to draw on the President's unlimited powers and open-ended perogatives. "Osagyefo says" or "Osagyefo wants" was all that was required to overcome resistance within the administrative jungle created by personal rule.

Taking a leaf from the book of the Communist Party, Nkrumah introduced into the administrative structure the concept of parallel directive power: Alongside the regular governmental agencies, ministries, and commissions, there would be political bodies covering identical spheres of responsibility. However, in the Soviet Union, the Party Secretariat, which seemed to be the general model for Flagstaff House, is indeed a Party agency. Nkrumah's secretariats, however, were outlets for personal power whose functions, more likely than not, would be exercised, when the urge came, by an *ad hoc* committee or council convened by Nkrumah on the spur of the moment.

Confusion by Design

There appears to be a little more to the confusion surrounding the operation of the personal-machine state than meets the eye at first glance. Erratic conduct of government and abrupt, flighty administration may be more than accidental by-products of personal rule; they may be part of a design. Confusion, uncertainty, unpredictability, inconsistency, and obscurantism may well be devices favored by the personal ruler for attaining and maintaining power.

In pursuing that technique, Nkrumah did not behave differently from any other leader who seeks to preserve a certain air of secrecy around his political purposes and activities. What is unusual, however, in the case of Ghana is the degree to which this confusion permeated all phases of government and administration.

In order to maximize his chance of political as well as physical survival, Nkrumah, in building the political machine, created, in part accidentally, but in part deliberately, an unfathomable administrative jungle. Some of his collaborators, certain that even he could not see through the maze he had created, attempted to cover up the deficiency by displaying to outsiders an air of certainty and self-assurance concerning administrative procedures, lines of responsibility, spheres of jurisdiction. But throughout government and administration, the rule seemed to be: "When in doubt, refer to Flagstaff House."

At Flagstaff House, Osagyefo's answer varied, the channels through which he ordered things done varied, the persons whom he wanted involved varied. No one was absolutely sure from day to day who was supposed to do what, when, and how. Nkrumah's practices confused friend and foe alike.

The confusion must be traced in part to the inexperience of staff members constantly subject to transfer and to reassignments, to the substantial increase in workload, and to Nkrumah's frequent insistence on resolution of insoluble problems and hopeless administrative tangles. However, Nkrumah appears to have fostered a certain amount of confusion in order to make himself indispensable and to frustrate efforts of internal and external enemies to assess or predict his intentions.

His practices made it all the more mandatory for elements wishing to overthrow the machine to direct their efforts to the source.

Construction of the personal political machine had been substantially completed by 1962. Finishing touches were applied between 1962 and 1965.

The adjustment from constitutional government to personal machine had been conducted mainly under the cover of ideological change, and under the misleading label of "one-party state."

Of course, many of the steps taken and institutions or procedures devised did not immediately produce all of the expected results. Many were initially designed to implement more long-range goals. What was of central importance, however, was that control over all principal pressure points in state and society had been transferred to Nkrumah. The machine, though not functioning perfectly in all respects, stood ready. But Ghana and the world were not. Ghana's economy was slowly grinding to an all-time low, and the world, including many erstwhile admirers in the other African states, was taking another, closer look at Kwame Nkrumah and his formula for progress.

V

The Final Year

Nineteen sixty-five was the first year when the personal political machine was fully legalized in Ghana. It had been incorporated in the constitutional structure under the label "one-party state." A constitutional amendment had legalized the machine's capture of the judicial branch of government. The armed forces, the police, and the security forces had been reorganized, reoriented, and placed securely—as securely as could be done—under Nkrumah's personal supervision and control.

LEGITIMACY AND LEGALITY

Karl Deutsch has noted that in a tighly controlled political system, certain messages take precedence over others because legitimacy has been bestowed upon them. He suggests that other messages, lacking legitimacy, are assigned lower priority or may be pigeonholed or completely ignored.[1]

The central, all-pervading fact of Ghanaian political life in 1965 was Nkrumah's undisputed monopoly of legitimacy—*vide,* the numerous references to him in the press and in virtually all political oratory as the "Fount of Honor," the "Father of the Nation," the "Founder," the "Leader," "Osagyefo," "His High Messianic Dedication," even "Nkrumah of Africa." In the sphere of government, his word alone regulated political thought, programs, directives, and laws. Unless a proposal, at whatever level, had his approval or could at least be assumed to have his approval, it was not legitimate.

What is crucial to an understanding of the machine as it actually operated is the fact that a message or a communication, to be acted upon in any ministry or agency, needed Nkrumah's stamp of approval, explicit or implicit, actual or alleged. The situation was aptly summarized by the Principal of Cape Coast College of Science Education, Mr. Bakhoum, when citing the order of precedence governing communications in his own country, the United Arab Republic. The occasion was a dispute between the government and a group of teachers who insisted that their contracts be honored. Discussing the need for immediate action on messages from Nkrumah, he confided: "In my country, when the government wants something done, one does not question, one does not quibble, one does not cite constitutional conventions or contracts. One does it, and does it immediately."

Although Nkrumah paid lip service to the role of the party, no one was more aware than the party leaders themselves of the total lack of legitimacy accruing to the party, to any of its organs (including the much cited Central Committee) , or to any of its leaders. Those who made the mistake of taking seriously Nkrumah's occasional deferential references to the leading role of the party—e.g., Ako Adjei, Adamafio, Crabbe—had a rude and painful awakening.[2]

As noted earlier, the party press habitually made similarly deferential—or ritualistic—references to the role and function of the party in Ghana. However, in the final analysis, when deviation from the Leader's word appeared to threaten, little time was lost before the readers were reminded that it was Osagyefo, and no one else, who would decide what was right and wrong.[3]

The 1960 republic constitution was the product of Nkrumah's will and not, as implied in Article 1, of the will of the people. By the time that constitution had been promulgated, Nkrumah had seized all powers necessary to impose his will on the state, enabling him to formulate "the people's will" as he saw fit. The people had no independent channels left to contest his authority; references to the right to cast votes in "freedom and secrecy" had no practical value. No provision of the constitution had effect if the President, endowed with all requisite powers of coercion and control, wished it set aside or ignored. All legalistic quibblings aside, restrictive phrases like "subject to the provisions of the Constitution," (Article 8, section 2), or "except as may be provided by law" (Article 8, section 4) had to be interpreted in light of the fact that the President possessed the power to amend the Constitution at will and dictate legislation to the captive National Assembly. By 1965, there was in Ghana no source of legality or legitimacy over and above Nkrumah; that was the real meaning of the appellation "Fount of Honor."

COERCIVE AND CONTROL POWERS

The 1965 *Annual Estimates* under the entry "Office of the President" show an allocation of £1.65 million for "Special Services" and another item of £1 million under "Contingencies," actually increased to £2 million.[4] Another £600,000 was allocated to "Special Services, construction works, vehicles and equipment" under "Development Expenditures." The total, more than £4 million, represented approximately 20 per cent of the total allocation for the Presidency, including a long list of appropriations for functions in administration and development. "Special Services" covered the secret police, the President's private, Russian-trained guard, security patrols, informers, wiretapping and other listening devices, detention apparatus, security walls around Flagstaff House, security-force buildings and fortifications at Presidential residences and offices, bullet-proof cars, and so on. All of these funds were at the sole discretion of the President, not to be accounted for to anyone. A considerable share of these funds were actually applied to various all-African projects and ventures, but without controls and frequently against civil-service advice.[5]

Having transferred the secret police to the Office of the President, Nkrumah was operational head of secret-police investigations.[6] The flow of information concerning the activities of cabinet ministers, party leaders, his own private secretary, judges, generals, and civil servants now reached him routinely and directly through an extensive apparatus of agents and informers. Endowed with powers of detention without trial or appeal, with the power to remove judges—in the event that a judge did the unexpected and lent himself to the questioning of a detention order—Nkrumah was now able to impress all who needed to be impressed with the importance of constant vigilance and absolute loyalty to him personally. Giving a personal warning every now and then to members of his staff who had been reported by the police to have "gossiped" about him, or to cabinet members reported to have questioned a presidential decision, Nkrumah was able to control even private conversations, not to mention official acts.

Where necessary, terror, including psychological pressure through invocation of juju practices, was applied. The wires in Nkrumah's hands controlling the state apparatus, and, equally important, also controlling the society in general by indirection, were now drawn quite taut.

Yet dictators are never quite secure enough. Additional steps had to be taken to tighten the security net. In August, 1965, Major General S. J. A. Otu, Chief of the Defense Staff, and his Deputy, Lieutenant General J. A. Ankrah, were abruptly dismissed and two lower-ranking officers were promoted to take their places. One issue may well have been that Otu and Ankrah had objected to the growth of what amounted to an extraconstitutional, private army controlled by Nkrumah. Reorganizing the Ministry of Defense, Nkrumah, as Supreme Commander of the Armed Forces, now assumed direct operational supervision of and direct personal responsibility for all military affairs. He even forbade the Minister of Defense to visit military installations without his authorization, a move designed to conceal the creation of the private army and the establishment of supporting strategic ammunition dumps throughout the country.[7]

All this was no more than a formalization of arrangements that had been in operation for some time. The Ministry of Defense had long since become a hollow shell. For some time prior to the changes, the top military command and the Minister had been routinely bypassed in the traffic of confidential messages between Nkrumah and his personal informants, the uniformed and civilian cogs in the political machine. As noted above, the Minister's prime responsibility had been to act as a watchdog over the proceedings in the politically harmless arena of the National Assembly.[8]

SUBSISTENCE CONTROL

The combination of what went under the name of development planning, socialist economic organization, and personal machine politics had extended Nkrumah's influence to the point where his subsistence control was complete for practical political purposes. Given the fact that the overwhelming majority of the Ghanaian population was economically wholly dependent upon marginal units of income that could be easily controlled, only a relatively minute group—mainly the pre-independence middle class—constituted a challenge to Nkrumah's desire to achieve total subsistence control over all segments of the population. But even the wealthy could not escape the dragnet of the personal machine.

The plethora of regulatory measures taken during the years of machine building and consolidation of power had handed Nkrumah a most effective arsenal of economic-political coercive weapons. By the end of 1965, he had at his disposal and used from time to time statutory control powers over any or all of the following: passports and exit visas, export and import licenses, foreign exchange, operators' licenses, land allocation, national and local regulatory powers in other spheres, granting of foreign and domestic contracts, loans and credit facilities, government employment, and foreign and domestic scholarships.[9]

Securely ensconced at the controls of a country-wide, all-encompassing web of power and influence, he also possessed and utilized the prerogatives of all bosses of political machines: economic blackmail, extortion, and bribery.

By the end of 1963, 39 per cent of all people employed in industry in Ghana were employed in "public authorities," firmly within reach of the personal machine through direct powers, the cabinet, regional commissioners, and local government. At that time, Ghana's total number of employed was 375,000. Of that total, 245,000, or somewhat more than 60 per cent, were in public enterprises. By the end of 1964, the share of public employees had risen to nearly 70 per cent of the total, or 261,900.[10]

With the passage of amendments to the Civil Service Act in September, 1965, all remaining barriers to wholly arbitrary dismissal by the President had been removed and subsistence control over the entire body of government employees was complete.

By March, 1965, forty-seven state enterprises had been created. The boards, as one quick glance at the rosters showed, had been staffed not with the most competent but with the most loyal (i.e., to the machine) friends and associates of the President, including a number of attractive but totally inexperienced women members of the National Assembly. Since these establishments were directly under the presidential State Enterprises Secretariat, headed by all-purpose Executive Secretary J. V. L. Phillips, thousands of employees and millions of pounds were at the President's mercy and disposal. They were no farther from his personal control than the nearest telephone. The efficiency-oriented staff members in the Secretariat who attempted to halt the drift to institutionalized incompetence and corruption were fighting a losing battle.

POLICY, DECISION-MAKING, AND PLANNING

Policy and Decisions

Perhaps, to do justice to the system of personal rule, the old, accustomed nomenclature of government and administration and some of the modern terms should be replaced by new terms reflecting the radically altered institutional and procedural concepts and arrangements. Terms like "executive," "legislative,"

"judiciary," "party," and "local government" suggest public functions, lines of communication, spheres of jurisdiction, responsibility, and accountability, and powers and prerogatives that
under personal rule either have become totally blurred or have
been abolished altogether.

Nkrumah had steadily assumed powers over *all* spheres of
government and administration until not one effective check
or balance remained to contest his will. Substantive distinctions
between the presidency and the cabinet, between these two
branches and Parliament, and between all three and the judiciary
had been wiped out. All branches of government and administration had been thoroughly and completely integrated and had
been reduced to mere administrative instrumentalities of the
presidency. The continued recognition of separateness in form
—in the constitution, in statutory arrangements, and in political
and administrative practice—were mere bows in the direction of
administrative exigency, more important, perhaps, in the direction of African public opinion and the opinion of potential investors in the economy. For a variety of reasons, personal rule
prefers to be called by another name.

Seeking to present a general outline of the formal governmental structure, the author of an article, "Organization of Government in Ghana" sketched, probably inadvertently, the true
state of affairs in the following descriptive summary:

> The Head of State as provided by the Constitution is a President
> who is also the Supreme Commander of the Armed Forces and the
> Fount of Honor. Subject to the provisions of the Constitution, the
> executive power of the State is conferred on the President. This
> *Executive* power may be said to be *exercised* in three main spheres
> [italics added]:
>
>   (i) Legislative
>   (ii) Judicial
>   (iii) Executive[11]

What had been the royal prerogatives of the Queen before
proclamation of the Republic had now been translated into a

system where Parliament and the courts had been incorporated into the executive branch of government. The author probably had not intended to be so blunt. In effect, Parliament, the judiciary, and the executive branch, but also the party and all of its auxiliary organizations, including the trade unions, had in political practice become appendages or departments in the personal political machine. They had been fashioned into instruments of personal rule, each used as the occasion demanded and frequently only for appearance's sake. If any of the several organs of personal rule were permitted from time to time to operate without direct presidential intervention, it was only because Nkrumah was too preoccupied—a state of affairs that provided opportunities for the civil service to correct some of his mistakes—or the situation simply did not warrant his special attention. What matters, however, is that the President had the undisputed power to impose his will upon any and all of the public organs of government and society and upon many of the private organizations as well.

Applied to the policy and decision-making processes, especially in the sphere of broad public policy, economic development, trade and commerce, security, social policy, and foreign affairs, that state of affairs meant a presidential monopoly. He delegated his powers as he saw fit and recalled delegated powers at will. He organized the supreme policy and decision-making apparatus as he deemed necessary and convenient, charts and organization manuals never quite catching up with the developments. Observation indicates that the administrators also had great difficulties catching up with the latest changes.[12]

One particular source of confusion was Nkrumah's reliance on alternating circles of advisers. Toward the end, there was no telling which adviser of the pool available or which group would be utilized by the President for a given purpose. To employ an expression used by Karl Deutsch, the decision-making system—if one may call it that—under personal rule is "nontransitive."[13] In a "transitive" system, A may have nominal precedence over

B and B over C. In the process of decision-making, the chain of precedence is observed. In the "nontransitive" system, while A may have nominal precedence over B, and B over C, C may be endowed with powers over A by fiat of the supreme ruler without alteration of the nominal order of precedence.

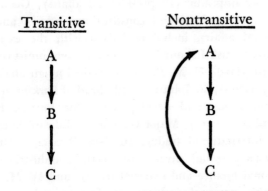

Given Nkrumah's reliance on administrative obscurantism, "nontransitivity" became the rule rather than the exception and official precedence meant little. Accordingly, the reference to the party as "the core of all organization of the people" had no practical significance.[14] The nominal ruling body of the party, given precedence over cabinet ministers in the official table of precedence published by direction of the President, actually could do no more than hope to be consulted from time to time.[15] The theorists writing in the official *Ghanaian Times* deluded themselves when they used the phrase "the party decides."[16]

A close look at who the President's principal advisers on policy really were reveals that party leaders, who had been deliberately selected for their comparatively limited intellectual capabilities, played only a marginal, decorative, or ritualistic role in the decision-making processes. The principal civil servants at Flagstaff House, imported special advisers and personal friends of sorts, seem to have been far more influential than any of the party leaders.

Most prominent among advisers in 1965 appear to have been James V. L. Phillips, (financial, economic, administrative), Michael Dei-Anang (African and foreign affairs, publishing), E. Ayeh-Kumi (Nkrumah's personal investments, external trade and finance), E. K. Okoh (the so-called Secretary to the Cabinet), T. K. Impraim (all presidential affairs), Geoffrey Bing (trouble-shooting, legal and constitutional affairs, and certain international affairs, including liaison with the extreme left wing of the British Labour Party and the Communist countries), D. N. Pritt (law), H. M. Basner (certain foreign affairs, publications, speeches), Sir John Howard (head of Parkinson Howard, Ltd.; construction and development), Sir Patrick Fitzgerald (trade and commerce), Major General Sir Edward Spears (mining and international trade), Dr. Noe Drevici, a Dr. Sargall (Nkrumah's personal investments, certain industrial projects, international finance and external trade), and W. M. Q. Halm (Nkrumah's personal investments, finance, mining, external trade). Professor William E. Abraham appears to have been one of the principal advisers, especially on higher education, communications, Nkrumah's publications and speeches, personnel policy, and some aspects of foreign affairs. There is strong evidence that the Soviet Ambassador had Nkrumah's ear in a number of areas.[17] And Sam Ikoku, a Nigerian, and Dr. Ekow Daniels appeared to play fairly significant advisory roles. There also was the "holy man" and a fetish priestess.

Among cabinet members, Minister of Finance K. Amoako-Atta, Minister of Education Kwaku Boateng, Minister of Justice Kwaw Swanzy, and Minister of Foreign Affairs Alex Quaison-Sackey seemed to have the edge over their colleagues. Kwesi Armah, Minister of Trade, could also be considered influential. Armah emerged toward the end as a key adviser, especially on matters related to Nkrumah's misappropriated funds.

Among the party stalwarts, aside from those already cited, the principal qualification for admission to the inner circle of advisers appears to have been willingness to serve not the party or some other organization but the political machine, to shrink into total political and personal subservience if not servility, to flatter, to spy, and to inform. Mediocrity appears to have been one criterion for selection. To speak of *advice* being rendered by these people would be inappropriate.

Nathaniel Welbeck, a singularly undistinguished political figure known for his disastrous diplomatic failure in the Congo[18] —and Martin Appiah-Danquah appear to have been members of the circle of intimates. Others were Kodwo Addison, S. W. Yeboah, A. K. Barden, A. E. Inkumsah, John Arthur, Kobina Hagan, J. E. Hagan, F. E. Tachie-Menson, J. S. T. Provencal, Kwaw Ampah, Kofi Batsa, Eric Heymann, Ambrose Yankey, Kofi Badu, T. D. Baffoe, Kwaku Akwei, and Krobo Edusei. In the main, these people were assigned errands for the President and functioned as watchdogs for the political machine in various spheres of government and politics—e.g., administration, national, regional, and local government, trade unions, farmers' cooperatives, the universities, the foreign service, the armed forces, and the police.

All advisers and all machine functionaries, regardless of status, had been conditioned by frequent examples to avoid making false assumptions concerning their positions, power, and influence. They were never allowed to forget the choke chain held by the President.

E. Ayeh-Kumi had been dropped during the purge following the 1961 strikes and disturbances and was in constant fear of his life. Michael Dei-Anang was frequently reminded of his principal political vulnerability: he was a product of the "imperialist" pre-independence civil service. So was J. V. L. Phillips. Both had to make special efforts to prove themselves, particularly their loyalty to Osagyefo. W. M. Q. Halm, like E. Ayeh-Kumi a genuine capitalist in CPP garb, needed to cling to Nkrumah to escape the socialist wolves. Alex Quaison-Sackey, having dared to eclipse Nkrumah on the world stage as President of the General Assembly of the United Nations, also needed to prove himself by special efforts.[19] So did Kwesi Armah, erstwhile Ghanaian High Commissioner in London, then Minister of Trade. Kwaku Boateng, who occupied the Ministry of Interior when the Preventive Detention Act of 1958 was extended in 1962, and Krobo Edusei, a lesser follower of Nkrumah's, were periodically reminded, through the controlled press and by direct personal admonition, that the sword of Damocles was suspended over their heads. Both had been accused of participation in one of the several conspiracies against Nkrumah.[20] Welbeck, Tettegah, and Baako had all been under fire and had all been saved repeatedly by Nkrumah's intervention; they knew that they owed their political life to him.

The extent to which Nkrumah would accept advice was governed in the main by these considerations: (1) he had to understand what was being communicated (in the sphere of economic and financial matters, his knowledge appears to have been limited); (2) the advice rendered had to contain a promise of advancing his personal interests and fortunes; (3) the ideas either had to be couched in social-revolutionary or Marxist terminology, and had to effectively conceal any traces of a bourgeois origin. The paradox suggested by this enumeration was characteristic of Nkrumah's behavior. Advice reflecting bourgeois thought or colonial mentality was eagerly accepted by him if patently related to the advancement of his personal interests. Unscrupulous capitalist businessmen could unload unprofitable projects merely by satisfying the personal-interest and social-revolutionary phraseology requirements. On the other hand, much useful and sound advice was either heavily discounted or entirely disregarded by him because it was proffered by persons whom he suspected of harboring bourgeois designs or who, in his opinion, had not yet shed the colonial mentality. This included Ghanaian businessmen, financiers, and civil servants. The foregoing explains the mixed nature of Nkrumah's circle of advisers. What emerges is a unique, personalized policy- and decision-making complex that was understood and accurately perceived, more or less, only by Nkrumah himself. The civil servants, outside the inner circle, and the remaining ministers, as well as the members of the party Central Committee, always uncertain as to who was making which decision, frequently had either to refer back to the President, which was as intended, or to temporize. Consequently, numerous decisions were simply not made or delayed endlessly.[21] The President's Office and Flagstaff House generally resembled a market place where presidential fiat was traded—genuinely presidential or just assumed or alleged—or where it was altered and adjusted. Sometimes it was simply sidetracked until recalled and forced to be implemented by direct presidential intervention.

A further element of confusion and uncertainty was introduced by Nkrumah's practice of governing by *ad hoc* impromptu directives, reflecting spur-of-the-moment interests, a sudden burst of enthusiasm, or an instinctive urge to appease a given faction, to please an interest group, to punish a rebellious or recalcitrant Member of Parliament—a vanishing breed—or to punish a community. Many of these abrupt decisions were empty gestures: There were no funds with which to carry them out.

Planning

If one accepted Nkrumah's multiple literary efforts and his speeches and formal addresses at their face value, it would appear that careful long-range planning were at the center of the program Nkrumah sought to implement. Indeed, a superficial glance at the formal structure of policy- and decision-making conveyed an impression that planning was of central importance. In mid-1965, directly under the President was an Office of the Planning Commission headed by an eminently qualified Executive Secretary and staffed by an impressive number of planning experts from a variety of countries. The office was under the nominal supervision of the State Planning Commission.[22] A Seven-Year Development Plan had been published and was supposed to be implemented in a series of annual plans.[23]

One economist found the Plan

> a clear expression of economic programmes as a function of national aspirations . . . matched by a sober—if perhaps optimistic—calculation of what can be achieved and what are the real resource constraints on development. As a result, the plan *is* a serious force both in the political drive behind its implementation and in the fact that its fulfillment—at least to, say, 80 per cent of output and 80–90 per cent of input targets—is attainable, barring radically unfavorable foreign-sector influences.[24]

Without any attempt to evaluate the purely economic aspects of this assessment, a follow-up of the economist's concluding reservation and of the general reservations necessary in regard to unfavorable internal-sector influences—i.e., influences flowing from the operations of the personal political machine—presents a somewhat different picture of planning in Nkrumaist Ghana. The description of planning, plan administration, and control in academic treatments, government manuals, and yearbooks appears to be quite unrelated to reality.[25]

Thus, long-range considerations of personnel, manpower recruitment, and resource planning were regularly thrown to the winds, increasingly so toward the end as a result of mounting economic pressure.[26] Such subtle essentials of planning as phasing—the inner logic governing each plan segment and dictating specific courses of action and prescribing appropriate administrative machinery—were regularly overridden by *ad hoc*, spur-of-the-moment decisions. These decisions, as likely as not emerging from a hastily arranged conference between Nkrumah and his Minister of Finance or a high-pressure salesman from one of the more highly industrialized countries, would change budget estimates, reallocate expenditures, transfer functions from one Ministry to another, change intra- and inter-agency allocations at will.[27] Major policy changes were made in this fashion regardless of provisions in the annual or long-range plans, frequently based on no research or systematic consultation whatsoever and disregarding the wholly subordinate, decorative planning, state control, and audit agencies and commissions. Nebulous projects, such as "continental planning" in the case of the 1965 budget, were allowed to influence changes in the estimates, including allocation of actual working capital to "basic-industry construction" although none of the existing plans had made provision for that at this stage.[28]

The impotence of the State Control Commission and the audit machinery and the fact that the authority to spend was granted by the President and not by Parliament and that obtaining a deficiency appropriation simply involved rushing through Parliament supplementary estimates with minimal discussion and no debate created a situation in which there existed no agency to limit expenditures or the scope of economic activity effectively. As one high planning official complained: "There exists machinery to add but not to control expenditures. We are not following the Soviet system for they have an effective control agency."

In general, with regard to economic and fiscal policy, Nkrumah's style of rule became increasingly less suitable for a planned economy. Mistakes in judgment, the rule rather than the exception because of arbitrary dictates, were "corrected" in 1965 by further extractions of wealth from the people, reduction in their living standard, forced savings, and various "contributions." The usual constraints on economic activity, such as profitability, availability of resources, markets, and manpower, did not seem to weigh heavily. Where internal resources were insufficient— and the margin for further extraction of wealth from the Ghanaian people was diminishing from year to year.—external credits, barter deals, medium- and short-term loans, from dubious sources if necessary and from the planning perspective, wholly unreliable and unpredictable, were marshaled to plug the holes.[29]

The resignation in 1965 of the Executive Secretary of the

Planning Commission was due largely to his realization that there were under the prevailing system of government no real prospects for planning or plan implementation in Ghana.

The situation concerning planning, policy-making, and administration was so notorious that a mission from the International Monetary Fund, sent to Ghana early in 1965 to investigate the climate for assistance from that source, insisted on certain reforms. In his May Day address, Nkrumah promised to initiate these reforms.[30] In the following months, under pressure as a result of further deterioration in Ghana's financial position, certain limited, relatively marginal adjustments were made. But nothing was done to attack the root of the problem.

Faced with total collapse, a runaway deficit, further reductions in the people's living standard, and snowballing shortages, Nkrumah, three weeks before his fall and nine months after his pledge of May Day, 1965, again promised reforms.

He promised to reduce the 1966 budget "to a level which can be supported by available revenue." There was to be a "rephasing" of some of the development projects "so as to reduce their impact on our total expenditure budget." Credit and foreign-exchange controls were to be improved. "Every pesewa" was to be "properly accounted for." "To this end," pledged Nkrumah, after years of virtually uncontrolled spending, "I have given directions that the Auditor General's Department should conduct a detailed scrutiny of all revenue and expenditure, and to expose all irregularities that may be committed in any sector of the economy." More than half of the 1966 budget was to be devoted to "productive investments."[31]

The promises of reform were of course mere gestures to satisfy the conditions set by the IMF mission. There was no prospect that the reforms would be carried out to the extent required by IMF standards. Exposure of "all irregularities" would of course have exposed first of all Nkrumah himself, then the party leadership, the trade-union functionaries, the leaders of the Farmers'

Council, the ministers and their wives, the functionaries of the state-owned Ghana National Trading Company, the Ghana National Construction Company, and so on. It would, in short, have blown apart the political machine.

POLICY EXECUTION AND ADMINISTRATION

Party and Nonparty "Bureaucracy"

One student of administration in developing countries notes: "After all, it is not very realistic not to consider the party bureaucracy as part of the public bureaucracy in a regime where the single party and the state are *claimed* to be one and indivisible [italics added]."[32] Aside from the error of mistaking claims for reality, the observer shows little awareness of practice under a system of personal rule. If, in Nkrumaist Ghana, the two bureaucracies were allowed to be merged, it was only at the politically relatively insignificant local-government level, where the functionaries could be separated into isolated groups and easily controlled. At the higher levels, by design, the party was kept apart from the civil service. To be sure, from time to time party spokesmen voiced their longtime grievances against the nonparty bureaucracy—voiced originally by Nkrumah himself.[33] Thus, one spokesman urged in 1965 that "party faithful" should be promoted, if necessary bypassing others in order to assure that people would be brought into controlling positions within the service who would assure implementation of "party policy."[34] Similarly, the Director of the Institute of Public Administration, a thoroughly frightened man because he was not a party member but a career civil servant, protested: "I firmly believe that a civil servant must be loyal to his Head of State and to his State, and his actions must be shaped to fit into this loyalty." He also urged that civil servants comply "with accepted socialist ideals of the African Governments."[35]

The practice in Ghana was quite different. The top civil servants (J. V. L. Phillips, for example, E. N. Omaboe, E. K. Okoh, and T. K. Impraim) cared little what the party—as distinct from the party leader—had to say, and directed their personnel in accordance with their own standards and criteria. Nkrumah actually encouraged civil servants in this posture of independence from the party as distinct from personal loyalty to him.

Two basic strategic considerations appear to have governed Nkrumah's concept of the administrative role of the party in the state: No major group was to be allowed to develop political power of its own, and no major group was to be provided with an opportunity to combine with any other major group—e.g., the party to merge with the civil service or with the army. Accordingly, the role of the party in the actual administration of the state was wholly subsidiary. It was but one of several instrumentalities employed by Nkrumah, and it was an exceedingly weak one, growing weaker as one went down the hierarchy. At the grass-roots level, it was virtually nonexistent as an effective arm of government. Its principal purpose appears to have been to provide attendants for mass rallies and demonstrations. As for the "party bureaucracy," it had no substance below the level of the district commissioner. The regional and district commissioners and the party "education officers" were part of the regional organization establishment which was also administered out of the President's Office. Their salaries were under the direct control of the President; so were their emoluments and privileges. They knew their role. They were expected to act as the eyes, ears, and mouth of the General Secretary of the Party, Kwame Nkrumah, and no more.

Although an elaborate CPP headquarters existed, party decisions and directives were more likely than not issued directly from Flagstaff House. Attempts by higher or lesser party leaders or members of the party bureaucracy to inject themselves into the administration of the other divisions in the President's complex of responsibilities brought forth swift and stern reprimands and corrective action. Hence, the frequent complaints in the press that ministers did not heed and civil servants sabotaged "party directives," acted in violation of "Nkrumaist ideology," and ignored the "revolutionary spirit."[36]

If the party must be related to the government, it must be viewed as no more than a hierarchy without solid following, without effective, competent middle- and low-level leadership, without a working bureaucracy. It was no more than an aggregate of factions carefully balanced and shrewdly manipulated by Nkrumah for his own ends.

Changing the Façade of the Party

Partly in response to domestic criticism by dissatisfied party faithfuls, partly to make the image of Nkrumaist Ghana more attractive to targets of Ghanaian propaganda elsewhere in Africa, Nkrumah late in 1965 gave in to demands for reform. But the reforms effected touched upon nothing of substance in the spheres of political power and influence. It was a mere face-lifting operation.

There were the usual references to political ritual: The party member was exhorted "to pursue a study of Scientific Socialism as enriched and advanced by Nkrumaism," and was asked to "remember that the Party is supreme and to do everything within his power to uphold this supremacy."[37] Clearly, this was not an invitation to overthrow the personal political machine. In the event that a member misunderstood this reference, there was the oath sworn upon admission to the party that committed the initiate to be faithful and loyal not only to the party but also to the "Leader, Comrade Osagyefo Dr. Kwame Nkrumah."[38] Several changes were made in the composition and mode of selecting members of the party's National Executive Committee. The significance of these changes was minimal since neither the National Executive nor the Central Committee, the former's "directorate," possessed powers independent from those exercised by Nkrumah personally as Secretary General of the party, Life Chairman, Commander-in-Chief, Head of State, Head of

Government, head of the secret police, Fount of Honor, etc.[39]

Although it was hardly worth the trouble, the Kwame Nkrumah Ideological Institute at Winneba was placed under "the personal guidance, control, and direction of Osagyefo."[40] The principal reason for this change was increasing complaints about the conduct of the Institute's graduates. Too many of them, taking their training seriously, had allowed their demands for power and influence to range too freely. Asking for immediate and practical recognition of what they assumed to be their special status, they had become a source of embarrassment and potential opposition to Nkrumah.

Party and Parliament

Beginning with the formalization of the "one-party state" in 1964, the party was gradually allowed to strengthen its representation, but not its control, over the National Assembly, until in August, 1965, all members of the Assembly were party members. Ironically, and most significantly, when the party was allowed to increase its representation in Parliament, the function of that body had become wholly marginal—perhaps merely ceremonial. Party and Parliament had become no more than cogs in the political machine.

None of the MP's intent on advancing criticism of the President were so naïve as to test the validity of any one of the several safeguards of Parliamentary freedom and integrity enacted in years past and still on the statute books and cited in learned articles and government handouts. For instance, Section 21 of the National Assembly Act of 1961 provided: "There shall be freedom of speech, debate, and proceedings in the Assembly and that freedom shall not be impeached or questioned in any court or place out of the Assembly."

Similarly, Section 29: 2a of the same Act provided that "it is a contempt of Parliament . . . for any person to endeavour, by means of bribery, fraud, or the infliction or threatened infliction of violence, restraint, or spiritual or temporal injury to influence

a Member in the exercise of his functions." By 1965, such practices of contempt had become the rule in Ghana, the President
himself being the principal violator.

The constant presence on the Assembly floor of Kofi Baako,
then Minister of Defense as well as Leader of the House, was
primarily to ensure observation of the immunity not of Parliament but of the President. His principal function was to keep
careless members from going too far in exercising their right to
criticize along well-planned lines of argument.

Even general criticism of sectors of government outside the
Presidency was discouraged because, by inference or implication,
it inevitably threatened to come too close to the Leader. Attempts by Members to revise downward the estimates of a CPP-
dominated City Council that had been proved to be riddled with
corruption were held "criminal and dangerous" and "contrary
to the interests of the Party."[41] Apparently, the President's judgment was involved since it was his budget estimate that was being
"debated."

Members of Parliament wishing to voice criticism of blatantly
corrupt practices in the government, clearly erroneous or mistaken policy decisions, or obviously faulty provisions in a government-proposed bill sounded more like petitioners pleading for
merciful consideration than like people's representatives advancing the claims of their constituents. Since the first Parliament
had met in August, 1956, there had never been a question of
voting down a government-proposed measure.

On the very few occasions when some kind of action was taken
in response to major criticism first voiced on the floor of the
Assembly, it was certain that a number of conditions had first
been met: (1) an abuse had been uncovered that benefited a
person or persons other than the President or anyone favored by
the President; (2) a need had been established for a public scapegoat in order to divert public attention from a major flaw in
administration; and (3) the cooperation of the President had
been secured to stage the appropriate debate, to allow a motion

of censure to be introduced, and to allow the press to publish the names of the hapless culprits.[42]

It appears that, for a while at least, Nkrumah was prepared to utilize the National Assembly as a pressure device to keep his ministers alert and to give the public an assurance of sorts that their grievances were being aired and considered.

Far more important than these carefully controlled criticisms was the fact that some of the most incisive measures—restricting freedom, increasing taxation, reducing pensions or other benefits, increasing workers' contributions to social security, etc.—were passed either without debate (at times, all three readings were completed in one day before any Member had had an opportunity to see, let alone read, the draft bill) or following desultory debate, where eloquent praise of the government's and the Leader's wisdom far outweighed critical analysis.[43]

Not once after the liquidation of the opposition party did any MP suggest outright that socialism might not be the best road to economic progress in Ghana. All that the handful of critical MP's were able to do was to nibble around the edges of the President's program, picking at socialism, Nkrumaism, and other objectionable features of the regime through subtle innuendoes and oblique humorous references. Most crucial in the relationship between Parliament and the President was the fact that the President, not the Parliament, controlled the legislative initiative. Even the impressive findings of the Assembly's Public Accounts Committee, published from time to time, were no more than voices in the wilderness until translated into legislation and/or presidential directives. But as executive in charge of legislation, Nkrumah followed his own counsel in his own good time.[44]

Early in 1965, as the deficiencies of the regime became ever more apparent and the opportunities for Parliamentary criticisms grew, Nkrumah addressed himself to the problem of terminating what he regarded as an increasingly troublesome relic of the past. There were mounting signs of dissatisfaction in the country: the workers were unhappy with the price structure, with increased contributions to the social-security program, and with increased taxation; unemployment had increased because of mismanagement of the state enterprises and poor planning of government expenditures in other fields; and the armed forces showed signs of restiveness.

Elements within the party were clamoring for the removal from the Assembly of MP's who had been elected at a time when strategic consideration had made it advisable to conceal, as they put it, the "socialist nature of the revolution."[45] Furthermore, still wanting to observe certain formalities associated with parliamentary democracy, such as membership in Parliament for all cabinet ministers, Nkrumah began to think of improving the caliber of MP's in order to enlarge the source of supply for more competent cabinet officers. Most important, however, he wished to reorient Parliament from an organ of criticism and embarrassment to himself to one closely attuned to his wishes. To that end, he proposed to a Delimitation Commission that in redrawing the constituency demarcations for the next Parliament, an effort should be made to bring party, Parliament, and local government into line.[46]

Furthermore, he directed that "in future, in addition to his duties as a Member of Parliament, every Member of Parliament shall be in some kind of regular employment."[47] Since Nkrumah was the principal employer in Ghana, this further reinforced machine control over Parliamentary debates. If that was not sufficient, he further directed: "In order to ensure that Members of Parliament faithfully discharge their responsibilities and obligations to their constituencies, the Central Committee of the Party will be empowered *by law* to unseat any Member of Parliament who in the opinion of the Central Committee has lost the confidence of the Party. [Italics added.]"[48] The "opinion" of the Central Committee was of course that of its undisputed Chairman.

At the same time, when a new, ever more pliable Parliament

was to be "elected," Nkrumah proceeded to close another hole in the screen protecting him from embarrassment. In the 1960 "referendum," he had been opposed for the Presidency by Dr. J. B. Danquah. Danquah, in spite of extensive harassment and restrictions, had been able to publicize the President's weaknesses and to criticize the regime in general. Accordingly, several bills regarding presidential election were designed to provide, among other things, that "in future only one person shall be nominated as candidate for President." There were the usual bows to legalism and formality, purporting to regulate the nomination procedure, but the main purpose was clear: Nkrumah had become tired of elections that, although invariably resulting in overwhelming victories for the CPP and him, had nevertheless provided opportunities for criticism.[49]

Desultory though it was, the debate on the bills brought out that because Nkrumah controlled admission to party membership and because the party membership card was now mandatory for candidacy and for membership in the National Assembly, the President could, by secret fiat, deny any citizen the right guaranteed by the constitution to be a candidate to represent the people in Parliament. What the remarks of one member brought to light, to the visible embarrassment of Kofi Baako and Nathaniel Welbeck was the fact that there existed no ascertainable criteria for admission to the party other than those decided upon from time to time by Nkrumah. Thus, the personal political machine was assured a monopoly of seats in a Parliament that, so it was broadcast across the continent of Africa, was the repository of the will of the people.[50]

Significantly, even though all of his hand-picked candidates were running "unopposed," Nkrumah canceled the election at the last moment. He had been advised that voters, now beginning to be restive, would express their dissatisfaction with the regime by boycotting the election in certain areas or, worse, by demonstrating against the regime in more articulate forms.[51]

Election or not, Nkrumah at last had his wish—a National

Assembly entirely of his own choice, though nominally the candidates had been "selected" by the Central Committee. Nkrumah's personal Parliament was now joined to his personal political machine.[52]

On August 24, 1965, Nkrumah was able to say to the new Assembly: "The days are gone when the Speaker sat like an umpire over the dissensions, bickerings, and parliamentary maneuvers of rival political parties. Ours is a House united by one Party, one ideology, one claim, one destiny."[53]

On September 10, the National Assembly passed the National Assembly (Amendment) Act, which included a provision permitting recall of a Member by either the electorate or the party if the Member "abused the confidence reposed in him at the election." But there had been no election; therefore, there was no electorate. We have also established that for purposes of independent initiative there was no party. There was only Nkrumah. Thus, what the change did was to dress up Nkrumah's already extensive powers, under Preventive Detention procedures, for instance, in a more legitimate garb, that of "popular recall." *The Ghanaian Times* promptly sent up a smokescreen to conceal the basic political purpose—namely, the advancement of the political machine:

> This is the finest example of the truth of Osagyefo's assertion that in Ghana the people are the repositories of power. They do not merely elect. They do not merely have a chance, on expiry of a constitutionally determined period, to either confirm or alter their choice. They also hold the power to withdraw their mandate from a representative who, between the constitutionally prescribed period, abuses their confidence.[54]

As a matter of course, the confidence involved and the abuses referred to related to the person and the office of the President.

By the end of 1965, there remained in the National Assembly only one critic of the President, S. I. Iddrissu. Although he studiously, often elaborately, concealed the ultimate target of his sharp attacks on the government, many of his sallies clearly implied criticism of the source of all power and responsibility. On August 30, 1965, he accused the Central Committee—and thus the Life Chairman/Secretary General—of removing "get-rich-quick" officials from their posts only to place them subsequently in higher positions. In particular, he was referring to a case of theft by a high official in Nkrumah's Security Service. Iddrissu was promptly cited before a subcommittee of the newly established Party Parliamentary Disciplinary Committee. Incorrigible, Iddrissu challenged the right of anyone to cite him for availing himself of what he considered his parliamentary privileges.[55] In February, 1966, Iddrissu was expelled from the party and thereby lost his seat in Parliament.[56]

ADMINISTRATIVE STYLE

The conventions, euphemisms, and formalities that cover up the true power and influence relationships in an administrative structure are quickly torn asunder under pressure of conflict and crisis. One such crisis erupted on March 27, 1965, in the sphere of relations between Nkrumah and the University of Ghana. Beyond its immediate implications for higher education, however, the crisis revealed the full extent to which regimentation of thought and practice were to be extended under personal rule.

We have noted earlier that during 1964 Nkrumah had made several moves to bring the University of Ghana, and higher education in general, to heel. These moves had included arrests of faculty members, deportations, mob scenes, threats to deny scholarships, veto of proposals for promotion, prohibition of controversial lectures and debates, etc. The moves had also included denying the Vice Chancellor, Conor Cruise O'Brien, direct access to the Chancellor—i.e., Nkrumah.

Following a series of provocations, the Vice Chancellor, believing that the final and crucial battle for the integrity of the University and of higher education was being joined, included in his annual report to the University congregation several references to the diminution of academic freedom during the preceding academic year. He also made reference to what he and the majority of the faculty viewed as highly arbitrary, if not unconstitutional, interferences by the President in the affairs of the University. He cited previous assurances by Nkrumah that academic freedom would be maintained. Since he was reporting to the University on official business, he also made specific references to correspondence between himself and Nkrumah, in the latter's capacity as Chancellor.

The viciousness of the ensuing press attack on the Vice Chancellor personally and the nature of the arguments employed must have been—in view of the controlled state of the Ghanaian press—authorized by the President. The press attack was sustained for seven days, filling two or three pages per issue, including editorials, commentaries, scurrilous and libelous letters of a type never permitted against personal appointees of the President unless Nkrumah had been consulted.

If there had been any doubt concerning the President's role in the campaign, this was dispelled when *The Ghanaian Times* published confidential correspondence between the Vice Chancellor and an official of another university, the correspondence having been obtained from the files of the Ministry of Education.[57] The implications of that move for all administrators in Ghana, for all administrative correspondence, were quite clear. But the personal-machine state does not know restraint. When provoked, its power is unleashed with uncontrolled fury. In the following passage, which appeared in *The Ghanaian Times* during the attack on the Vice Chancellor, all administrators, all government employees, and in fact all citizens and noncitizens in Ghana were put on notice that any criticism of the President, however expressed, direct or indirect, was liable to bring the offender into conflict with the Criminal Code:

Any Vice Chancellor (who is but Osagyefo's caretaker) who exposes the Chancellor to *unfavorable comment, criticism,* or ridicule *either in open convocation, in Committee, or private conversation,* is guilty of disrespect to the Chancellor, and for that we have an Act of Parliament. [Italics added.][58]

One reason for the uncontrolled fury behind the press attack was the fact that Conor Cruise O'Brien, a man of considerable international stature, posed too big a political obstacle for simple deportation. However, lest anyone failed to take the numerous hints merely because the target of the attacks had not been removed from the country, the article added this warning:

We think it necessary to say that Ghanaians *in high political and civilian* positions should not play with fire by entertaining socially these academic assassins. . . . Osagyefo has warned us that what imperialists cannot do by negotiation they will achieve through cocktail parties and mental subversion. [Italics added.][59]

Once more, the instrument of social ostracism was being invoked. Such was the administrative style of the personal political machine.

Following the departure of O'Brien, after his contract had expired, Nkrumah selected a more compliant officer to occupy the top administrative post in the politically critical University. His choice, duly ratified by the faculty, was Professor Abraham, chairman of the presidential book-censorship committee, a probable co-author of Nkrumah's *Consciencism,* and vigorous exponent of Nkrumaism. (In fairness to Professor Abraham, it should be recorded that he never gave me the impression that he really believed in the nonsense he propounded; this was also true of most of Nkrumah's other ideologists.)

On December 9, 1965, Nkrumah returned to the theme of academic freedom in an address honoring one of his expatriate friends, Dorothy Crawfoot Hodgkin, wife of Nkrumah's long-time friend and adviser Thomas Hodgkin, who had recently received a Nobel Prize for her work in chemistry. Observed the President: "Gone are the days of such shibboleths as art for art's sake, knowledge merely as an end itself, and the pursuit of truth solely for its own sake."[60]

From now on, knowledge and truth were to be "socially relevant"—i.e., they were to be at the disposal and the mercy of the personal political machine.

COMMUNICATIONS AND IDEOLOGY

The Media

In June, 1965, in response to questions by a Nigerian interviewer, Nkrumah advanced the thesis that in Ghana the press was free:

> We have several papers, each with its editor. These editors, I dare state, are among the freest and fiercest editors in the profession of journalism today. Once a week they meet *with all agencies* of the State and Party connected with publicity. They freely discuss home and external affairs. After this, each editor is free to choose both the subject and the presentation of his editorial.
>
> In Ghana, ownership of the Press is vested in the state and the organizations of the people, *making the national interest always supreme.* [Italics added.][61]

In the light of the actual state of power and influence in Ghana, these remarks could be interpreted as follows: The principal editors, as noted above, were owned by Nkrumah, who had trapped them into accepting government housing for which they paid, at most, only a nominal sum. The press was owned by the state as personified by the President's Office in the person of the publicity secretary, who supervised, among other things related to communications media, the organization set up specifically to control the press. The editors were free to discuss all internal and external affairs that did not reflect adversely upon the person and acts of the President. Since all matters of substance in Ghana were in one or another way traceable to the President, very little of substance was left for the press to discuss without explicit presidential approval. In Ghana, the President, and not the press, determined the nature and limits of "the national interest."

The real situation was expressed fairly openly in an editorial in *The Ghanaian Times:*

> Our socialist society cannot, and would not, tolerate the publication of any newspaper in Ghana which departs from the ideology and *loyalties* demanded from the press in socialist and *Nkrumaist* Ghana. Under these circumstances, there cannot be any real competition or difference in fundamental views between the *Graphic,* the *Ghanaian Times,* the *Evening News.* [Italics added.][62]

The reference to fundamental views, in the case of Ghana, must be translated as a reference to President Nkrumah's views, as clearly intimated by the words "loyalty" and "Nkrumaist Ghana."

Any competition between the several papers was barely perceptible and then only between the *Graphic* and the three major daily and weekly papers. Such controversies as were allowed in the press concerned matters of no substantive political import. Occasionally a cabinet minister was attacked, but the attack always stopped short of tracing responsibility to its known, logical end; it never even hinted at complicity at the top. Of course, any action taken on a matter raised in the press—e.g., pressure for the removal of a weak minister—occurred only if the President gave the sign.

Although the vague ideological prescriptions and warnings and the moralizing presidential addresses published in the press from time to time were largely ignored, some practical hints contained in these messages were undoubtedly taken seriously by what might be called the "influenceables." These segments, especially those in public positions, prone to adjust their behavior to official or societal prescriptions, saw in the press the writing on the wall, the presidential writ. But, by the same token, the journalist agents of the political machine studiously avoided trespassing upon the presidential preserve and loudly busied themselves with denunciations of relatively trivial transgressions, Lebanese businessmen, a hapless lesser minister or two, or a poor Ghanaian trader driven by the sagging economy to overpricing by one penny a carton of soap powder.

The conduct of the press might appropriately be described as a "catch-the-thief" campaign intended to divert public attention from the country's more fundamental problems. In this campaign, the sins committed by the colonial regime initially played a most prominent part. As that theme gradually faded, new rationales and new diversionary slogans and themes had to be devised. "Neocolonialism," "imperialism," and anti-Americanism emerged as handy substitutes.[63]

One problem facing the press was caused by the President's personal conduct—his luxurious living, ostentatious entertainment, immodest public posture, and personal financial dealings with shady foreign businessmen. The press solution was to ignore this completely and attempt to smother public misgivings on the subject by building up the President as the very fount of honor, morality, propriety, and modesty. Much of that effort centered on the President's celebrated "Dawn Broadcast" of April 8, 1961, an early-morning admonition to the people staged in the tradition of a tribal chief. (The prime target for the broadcast had been corrupted party leaders, cabinet officers, and government employees, and it contained specific proposals concerning proper personal conduct in a socialist society, as well as specific guidelines and standards for officeholders.) To the embarrassment of objective Ghanaian officials, this effort, as was inevitable, took the form of uninhibited sycophancy.[64]

Did the presidentially controlled Ghanaian press perform any of the functions ascribed by academic theorists to the press in less developed areas?[65] In particular, did it "mobilize," "modernize," and "educate"? And if it did, did it therefore, in the setting of personal rule, perform vital functions justifying its sycophantic, diversionary orientation?

No matter what circulation figures showed, there is no evidence that the press either reflected public preferences or actually reached the reading public with its messages—i.e., that these messages actually penetrated the language and perception screens, let alone affected the behavior of the reading public. In other words, if Nkrumah had really intended to employ the press in order to mobilize the public, he would have had to: (1) employ editors more highly trained in communications skills and less in the ritualistic and sycophantic arts; (2) order a real effort to discover the actual public interests, aspirations, and perception potentialities; and (3) act as a model for the public to emulate. There were no indications whatever that any of these prerequisites of an effective social-mobilization effort were being contemplated. Instead, Nkrumah favored journalists totally lacking in credentials as communications specialists; H. M. Basner, a refugee from South Africa, whose main concerns lay outside Ghana; Patrick Sloan and Dennis Ogden, two ideologists from Great Britain whose interests in life were wholly unrelated to Ghanaian public interests; and Sam Ikoku, an exceedingly intelligent Nigerian refugee. None of these could be expected to make an impact on Ghanaian public opinion. What was left of Ghanaian journalists was a handful of young men: Kofi Badu, Kofi Batsa, T. K. Baffoe, Eric Heymann. Their crude language in terms of Ghanaian psychological needs and socially irrelevant and often childish concepts of state, society, and the world were allowed to shape communication policy for Nkrumah.

Similarly dysfunctional for mobilization in Ghana were the simplistic efforts to present to the Ghanaian reading public the sophisticated views of academicians from the Soviet Union and the East European countries. These presentations on Marxism, Leninism, socialist planning, philosophy, and world politics were wholly extraneous to the social concerns of Ghana.

In Nkrumaist Ghana, mass mobilization was a wish, not a practice. The principal functionaries lacked both the required concepts and the instrumentalities. It is doubtful that Nkrumah, because of reasons related to maintenance of his personal rule, would actually have tolerated development of an effective machinery for mass mobilization. Moreover, the careless use of words by editors and writers and the absence of an effective communications infrastructure would indicate strongly that planned social action, socially relevant to a significant degree, could not be and was not possible in the Nkrumaist setting.

There seemed to be no more than an infrastructure for the satisfaction of the President's personal perception of what needed to be done—a kind of incestuous communication from President to press and back to President—and for the momentary stimulation of excitement among a very limited segment of the public, mainly in the poorer section of Accra.

Nkrumaism—1965

After nearly a decade of Nkrumaist rule, not counting the years preceding independence, what was the practical political and social content of the impressive body of ideological formulation produced by Nkrumah, or produced in his name? As I have indicated, I find its nature to be opportunistic, uncoordinated, unprincipled, nebulous, and open-ended. Its major social purpose related to Nkrumah's and his subalterns' needs for a respectable rationale to cover up the malfunctions of personal rule.

In March, 1965, eight years after independence, the "ideological" pace setter of Nkrumaism, *The Spark*, cited "three books [which] taken together give us a theory and philosophy of development that show how the New African can achieve a fast rate of all-round development within the context of full independence."[66] The books referred to—Nkrumah's *Africa Must Unite, I Speak of Freedom*, and *Consciencism*—do nothing of the sort.

There is no inherent connection between the outpourings of Nkrumah, largely directed at an imaginary all-African rather than a purely Ghanaian public, and social planning in and for a developing society. The final chapter of *Consciencism* claims the impossible:

> So alert can positive action be, alert to all negative possibilities, and prompt under the guidance of an ideology to deal with these possibilities, that the course of positive action can be mapped out in set theoretic terms. For this a minimum number of initial symbols are necessary.[67]

The following formula is then offered to "demonstrate" the need for Nkrumaist positive action to secure a liberated African territory from the dangers of neocolonialism:

$$UGi \longleftrightarrow (pa^{\nearrow} + na)$$
$$\searrow$$

where $\quad\quad\quad\quad\quad$ O *Gi*

Gi	is	a liberated territory
U	is	united
pa	is	positive action
na	is	negative action
$\nearrow$	is	on the increase
$\searrow$	is	on the decrease
$\longleftrightarrow$	is	if and only if [68]

On August 24, 1965, Nkrumah, in an address to the new National Assembly, said: "We must know what we are doing and why we are doing it, in every phase of our efforts."[69] The very concept of separating the strategic and tactical requirements of the revolutionary, pan-African unity movement from public discussions, of concealing revolutionary objectives from the prying eyes of "neocolonialist" enemies of the revolution, of concealing from public view the private and personal affairs of the Leader, of actually outlawing discussions of matters related to the Leader, suggests that what Nkrumah really meant was that the public was to "know" one set of objectives and the ruler was to pursue another. Applied to ideological mass mobilization or articulation, this meant that Nkrumaist ideology was not a coherent whole, not a firm, identifiable set of ideas, social concepts, and prescriptions, but a propagandistic device to convey to the public a sense of purpose not necessarily related to what was actually transpiring at the policy- and decision-making levels. Nkrumaist "ideology" was, to fall back on an appropriate source, Marx, the "opium of the people."

Despite all academic findings to the contrary, the "system" of personal rule appears to be psychologically and politically incapable of settling on a firm set of ideological concepts, prescriptions, or methods. By its very nature, it is secretive and obscurantist. It must keep in a state of imbalance all serious efforts to develop ideological restraints; it must conceal its revolutionary objectives (giving it the best possible interpretation) or prevent formation of oppositional elements (its most probable political motivation).[70]

The vacuity of Nkrumah's thoughts on man and society must be fully appreciated before myth overtakes reality. The tendency of some students of ideology to mistake the appearance for the substance has diverted attention from the emptiness of Nkrumaism. The same applies to certain other variants of socialism in Africa today. The vast gap separating ambitious pronunciamentos and party manifestoes from political practice is too easily bridged by the uninformed reader of treatises on certain forms of African socialism, who casually assumes that the pronunciamentos are socially and politically relevant. It is far more likely that only the vacuity, the ambiguity at best, is socially of major relevance. Only the undefined or undefinable social doctrine can survive the trials posed by the irrationality, inconsistency, and subjectivity of personal rule; what is relevant is the general direction of social policy. But because it is so general, its application so very carefully shrouded from public inspection by the secrecy generated by personal rule, anything at all can be included under that broad cover.

The clearest indication of Nkrumaism's true nature may be

found in the following extract from an editorial on party unity
in *The Ghanaian Times* reverting once again to the "Left-Right"
juxtaposition:

> Nothing is more removed from Party reality, more injurious to Party
> unity, and *indeed more capable of undermining loyalty to our Leader*
> than the thought of right wing and left wing trends within the Party.
> This cannot exist and ought not to be contrived.
>
> Our Party is a revolutionary movement *with one ideology, Nkruma-
> ism,* and *one Leader,* Osagyefo Dr. Kwame Nkrumah, *from whom the
> Party derives its ideology.*
>
> In order to belong to it and be true to it, *one must fall in line
> with the Leader,* accept the ideology in its fullest depth, and *close
> the mind to all thought alien to his.* . . .
>
> The first thing we ought to do therefore in invoking ideological
> unity is to assert the *indivisibility of Nkrumaism* and *the supremacy
> of the Leader as the sole source of our ideological orientation.*[71]

REGIONAL AND LOCAL GOVERNMENT

In a less-developed country, all levels of government and administration below the central level are very much at the mercy
of the central government. This is true for a variety of reasons,
but it is primarily due to lack of funds and of the physical power
needed to overcome pressure from above. The lack of experience
and adequately skilled personnel contributes to that weakness.
Under the system of personal rule, the weakness becomes empha-
sized even more.

By 1965, Nkrumah had successfully integrated regional and
local government into his personal political machine. He had
achieved that primarily by making the regional commissioners
responsible to him directly and personally and by creating, under
them, a hierarchy of party attachés and political-education secretaries, all of whom were paid from government funds and were
part of the "establishment." The regional commissioners themselves were paid out of the Consolidated Fund under the budget-
ary rubric "President."[72] Coordination of the activities of the

regional commissioners centered on the Office of the President, which jealously guarded that sensitive line of communication, allowing no other rival center or gathering point to be established.[73] Again, given the wholly passive role of the party—even *The Ghanaian Times* had admitted that it was a purely executive instrumentality of personal rule—the regional organization and the party organization, although nominally linked at all levels, were strictly speaking separate instruments of presidential power. Both channels were open to the President, and Flagstaff House used these channels as the President saw fit. The several reorganizations on the regional, district, and local government levels, including the administrative structure of the local and municipal councils, merely reflected changing emphasis concerning the form of local government. The substance of control was never in doubt: All threads ran together into the hand of the President.[74]

VI

Evaluation: The Effects of Personal Rule on Government and Administration*

Personal rule appears to be regarded by vast numbers of people as a panacea. In times of stress or frustration, the Americans, the French, the Germans, and of course the Russians and the Chinese have submitted to one or another form of it. Now it is the turn of elements in the African states to succumb to the illusion of security under personal rule—the illusion of efficiency, stability, and progress. Brushing aside the alleged benefits suggested by political sympathizers and partisans, as well as academics, what can one conclude to have been the effect of personal rule on the government and administration of Ghana?

Political philosophers, theorists, and practitioners disagree on the role, function, and purposes of government. In the final analysis, a decision is based upon one's philosophy and perhaps one's social and political objectives and one's biases. At any rate, it is readily conceded that the following evaluation of the over-all effects of personal rule on Ghana is subjective. Neither the study nor the conclusions are meant to be definitive.

Admitting frankly that my selection is arbitrary, but not more

---

* The emphasis on Nkrumah's impact should not be taken to suggest that he was solely responsible for all the adverse consequences of Nkrumaist rule. Because the focus of this study is the personal political machine and because of the overpowering influence wielded by Nkrumah over his associates, exclusive consideration of his personal impact and his personal style would seem to be justified.

so than any other, I base my analysis on the effect of personal rule on four critical sets of governmental functions in a developing society: learning and correcting; regulating, ordering, and stabilizing; economic development; and ideological, moral, and aesthetic leadership.

In general, it is the purpose of government to maximize in a just and equitable manner the potentialities of the people to fulfill their basic objectives. To that end, government must promote the fullest utilization of the available human and material resources. The four functional areas deal with the responsibilities assumed by government in fulfilling its fundamental purposes.[1]

THE LEARNING AND CORRECTING FUNCTION

Clearly, maximum utilization of resources requires the fullest possible development of the society's critical faculties and collective brain power and the ability to bring this power to bear on the governmental functions. Borrowing a concept from cybernetics, it may be said that a government learns by performance, correcting its actions as information on performance is fed back into the system. The ability of a government and an administration to improve, to innovate, to modernize, in all spheres of responsibility depends on the extent to which information is received by the decision makers, the quality of that information, and the extent to which it is blocked or lost in transit as it passes through the channels of communication.[2]

As has been shown, personal rule, instead of maximizing the information, learning and correcting capacity of the system, maximizes the corrosive elements in society, progressively creating new sources of confusion, multiplying the opportunities for information to be blocked, lost, or diverted. Personal rule actually constitutes a major obstacle to the free flow of information required, partly because the ruler insists on imposing his own severely limited views upon the entire governmental and administrative machinery.

In the sphere of public administration, between 1951 and 1957,

Nkrumah constructed his own channels of communication to counteract what he regarded as retarding, obstructionist influences from expatriate holdovers from the colonial administration. He justified these measures as necessary to assure rapid progress in all sectors. The dynamics of personal rule, however, quickly reduced what originally may have been commendable, administratively sound aims to shoddy political maneuvers designed primarily to protect the personal political machine. Consequently, instead of an efficient network of communication channels, a series of *ad hoc* arrangements precariously dependent for guidance and control upon the limited capacities of one single human being were permitted to spread throughout the top policy- and decision-making agencies, condemning the state apparatus to thrash about aimlessly, to waste the available human and material resources. This applied across the board to all areas of government responsibility.

It is difficult enough in a developing country to obtain reliable data on the national level. Nkrumah, however, opted to abandon the near for the far, the manageable though difficult for the unfathomable. To achieve his ambitious continental objectives, he harnessed the scarce Ghanaian informational skills in the Foreign Ministry, the African Affairs Secretariat, and the universities to international will-o'-the-wisps, while sorely needed data on the ailing national economy awaited collection, processing, and accurate assessment.

Personal rule meant overvaluation of particular data that happened to strike the interest, curiosity, or fancy of the ruler. At times, the entire apparatus was directed to pursue a whim suggested to the ruler by whoever happened to have his ear. The information machinery was clogged with highly exaggerated data, or with memories of the colonial experience, of threats flowing from the various forms of imperialism that Nkrumah had designated as major threats to the security of Africa, and of the whole gamut of real and imagined threats to the security of the political machine at home. The collective brain power

of Ghana's intelligentsia, or the portion still available, was forced
to subscribe to Nkrumah's simplistic concepts of the processes
of history, his highly one-sided perception of the forces that pro-
pelled or resisted the African independence movement, and his
egocentric perception of what was required to advance the cause
of African unity. As a result, the learning and correcting capacity
of the government and administration of Ghana was submerged
in a welter of irrational, contradictory, erratic, highly emotional
perspectives concerning events at home and abroad: The learning capacity of Ghana was reduced to the learning capacity of
Kwame Nkrumah.

The sharp deterioration in the capacity to learn and to correct was in part the result of Nkrumah's tendency to purge his
environment of intellectually superior, and most important, in-
dependent-minded individuals. Nkrumaist Ghana probably more
than any other African state became a prime source of supply
of top-level administrative, journalistic, diplomatic, academic,
and professional escapees who preferred service abroad to service
under Nkrumah. In addition to those who served in New York,
Geneva, Addis Ababa, and elsewhere, far too large a share of
the country's intelligent citizens, rather than submit to the arbitrary rule, voluntarily retired from public life.

Nkrumah's persistent course in the direction of the Communist countries also contributed to the loss of learning and
correcting capacity. Although nominally committed to a diplomatic policy of nonalignment, he was actually delivering Ghana
into the economic, political, and military grip of either one or
both of the major Communist powers. The effect of this was felt
most severely in the gradual loss of expertise from the Western
states and the substitution of expertise from the Soviet Union,
Communist China, and the East European countries. Though on
the whole technically competent, too great a percentage of these
experts were seriously deficient in language and familiarity with
local conditions. The massive introduction of these elements into
the information channels of Ghana was like insertaing a scram-
bling device into a telephone system.

More generally, to use a phrase coined by Arthur M. Schlesinger, Jr., Nkrumah's personal rule undertook the process of removing Ghana from the "world of choice," where governments make decisions and the people take options from a range of possible alternatives, to a world of little or no choice.[3]

THE REGULATING, ORDERING, AND STABILIZING FUNCTION

One notion that has slowly spread in academic circles, mainly in the United States, is due for sharp revision—viz., that government and politics can be viewed as sets of activities or modes of behavior that take place within a "system." There is no reason why the term "system" cannot be used to describe the entire complex of government and politics. However, a serious problem arises when the notion of a system is allowed to control one's idea of the actual processes of government and politics. It is misleading to conclude thereby that in Nkrumaist Ghana certain "inputs" resulted predictably in certain "outputs."

Studying the government and politics, in particular the regulatory function ascribed to government in Nkrumaist Ghana, may be likened to following the famous croquet game in *Alice in Wonderland,* except that in the Nkrumaist setting, the objective was not only to frustrate the players but also to confuse the onlookers.[4]

Thus, one contribution by Kwame Nkrumah to the study of government and politics in a developing country, or to the study of the development of politics, is the demolition of the notion that the concept of a system—or of straight, linear progression—can be a key to understanding the personal political machine state. Alas, the over-all effect of Nkrumah's rule on Ghana has had more far-reaching and more profound, perhaps tragic, consequences. Instead of developing the regulatory function of government during his rule, he disrupted and stunted it. Instead of developing the necessary institutional structures, he mainly promoted what Samuel Huntington calls political decay.[5]

Professor W. Arthur Lewis, writing on the one-party state, notes: "One of the odder claims made for the single-party system is that it offers stable government. . . . This is not so. West African single-party government is highly unstable. Where opposition is illegal, governments can be changed only by *coups d'état*." He goes on to say that efficiency is required to root out the opposition but that no West African government commands that efficiency. Consequently, the inevitable conflicts and tensions are not removed but merely redirected. "All the tensions and conflicts of the society come to be concentrated in the struggles of the upper hierarchy of the party, whose members become identified with conflicting interests and policies. When these tensions become too great, the leaders turn upon each other, with deadly violence."[6]

The one-party state or system is a myth, certainly as far as Nkrumaist Ghana was concerned. Instead, there was a tightly controlled personal political machine. The very fact that the ruler in that setting personally and directly controlled and supervised elite recruitment and selection through a personalized arrangement of rewards and punishments enabled him to control the free flow of thoughts in the upper ranks of the party leadership. The situation did not permit "freedom of movement" and "prestige" to accrue to plotters and conspirators in the party, as Professor Lewis suggests.[7] Nkrumah succeeded in reducing the capability of party leaders to generate their own political force and influence. He accomplished that by selecting only mediocrities for subleadership functions, by devising obstacles to freedom of movement, by monopolizing all sources of prestige, and by keeping all leadership elements constantly off balance. The opposition of which Professor Lewis speaks existed, but not in the relatively powerless CPP.

Considering that Kwame Nkrumah was in power for fifteen years (including the period prior to independence), and assuming that stability means "a state of affairs that permits a political system to function without subjection to political changes not in accordance with the accepted and established rules or formulas," one can hardly say that his rule had no stability whatsoever.[8] But it was the stability of the prison camp, and it was short-lived, measured by the durability of other personalized regimes such as those of a Tubman, a Trujillo, or a Chiang Kai-shek. Violence and disorder, or the threat of violence, can be expected in the wake of independence in any underdeveloped society. Whatever government emerges, the odds are overwhelmingly against immediate success in the effort to close the development gap.

Certainly, all signs indicate that a multiparty system or a fractured political universe in which unlimited numbers of political cliques and cabals compete for power, spells unrest and insurrection in a underdeveloped state. Even if internal elements should combine to assure a modicum of stability and order, external financial and political influences would have a field day with some of the most likely weak and venal groupings. Nkrumah can claim some credit for reducing or minimizing the opportunities for nefarious foreign intervention, a constant threat to small, newly emergent states. But he did not succeed in eliminating all foreign intervention, and most important, he did not succeed in surviving politically himself. When one considers the cost to Ghana of Nkrumah's temporary success in endowing the state with short-lived stability, one cannot be too sure that the instability of a relatively open society would not have been to greater advantage.

After the coup, Nkrumah's financial adviser revealed that shortly before the end the President had made a will. He had consigned his ill-gotten fortune of at least £2.5 million to the CPP.[9] But he had left neither a political heir nor the machinery to facilitate orderly succession; the constitutional succession provisions were of no political consequence whatever since they failed to reflect the political reality.[10]

Instead of institution-building to facilitate orderly government and politics, personal rule places a premium on constructing institutions and developing procedures to assure the survival of the machine and the individuals upon which it depends. Part of the fierce loyalty displayed by some of Nkrumah's followers merely reflected a deep commitment to personal rule as an insurance against political death. "Rally around the leader" became an absolute necessity, and much energy was spent institutionalizing that principle, providing an entirely false focus for governmental and political activity—or "pseudo-political activity," as one scholar would call it.[11]

During the fifteen years he dominated the Ghanaian political scene, Nkrumah dismantled the institutional framework—the framework that restrains or keeps within bounds the disruptive and centrifugal forces, the corrupt politicians, the cliques, the cabals, found within any society or state.[12] Preoccupied with the requirements of the political machine, Nkrumah—as distinct from other sources of leadership—bequeathed upon his successor regime no other restraints at the national level than those embodied in a number of incorruptible non-Nkrumaist Ghanaians trained at Sandhurst and the British Police Training School at Hendon, as well as incorruptible elements in the civil service, the judicial service, and at the universities.

It was one of the many ironies of the Nkrumaist regime that the political machine, instead of mobilizing the intellectual resources of Ghana to develop truly African institutions and procedures, confined itself to inventing superficial political ritual as a backdrop for imported, second-hand institutions and procedures—imported, incidentally, from the Communist countries at a time when fundamental changes there had rendered the exports impractical and obsolete at home. Moreover, as applied to Nkrumaist Ghana, the discarded institutions and practices assumed comic, pseudo-socialist characteristics that not even the Communist advisers could take seriously.

The most striking illustration of this total failure to perceive that different cultures require different symbols was Nkrumah's attempt to duplicate in Accra the Red Square of Moscow. His Black Star Square, with its colossal reviewing stand and other trappings, stood as a monument to misplaced symbolism and misapplied "culture" transfer. The political-psychological value of that expenditure and many similar ones could not have amounted to very much.

Still another victim of personal rule was constitutionalism—or, to remain realistic, a dedication to constitutionalism. In particular, given the country's lack of tradition and experience in the more sophisticated aspects of modern government, it would have been too much to expect any form of government to devote much time and effort to the faithful and abiding maintenance of elaborate juridical defenses, such as the rule of law. Nkrumah's fault, however, was not that he failed to abide rigorously by the rule of law and the other pillars of constitutionalism, but that he destroyed the legal foundations, however weak, left by the British. We know the reasons for this failing, but it still needs to be underlined.

In practical political terms, Nkrumah's approach to power, crude and ruthless when his interests so dictated, revealed the basic aspect of law and legal practice in an underdeveloped social setting—namely, that law is no more than an instrumentality of political power. It has no power of itself. Its force potential is wholly derivative, not original. In a developed system, legal institutions, by force of tradition, custom, precedence, and the combined operational effects of socially mature and viable competing groups, acquire power and influence of their own. But in Nkrumaist Ghana, the courts, the legal profession, and legal scholarship were unable to escape political pressure. In the end, law and justice had been reduced to little more than handmaidens of personal rule.

As far as the public was concerned, the effects were devastating. Professor William B. Harvey, in his penetrating analysis *Law and Social Change in Ghana,* writes:

Whether fully supported by fact, the belief is prevalent that the courts who administer "justice" to the great mass of the population are in fact for sale to the highest bidder. The recent constitutional changes and the related actions of the President and dominant Party strike directly at the confidence in the integrity and independence of the superior courts.[13]

Similarly, it is necessary to stress the failure to instill in the youth of Ghana a sense of political integrity, civic devotion, and dedication to public life. The bogus philosophy of *Consciencism*, the well-meaning but substantially irrelevant prescriptions advanced by the lecturers from Moscow and Leningrad, the frauds perpetrated by pseudo scholars from Great Britain and the United States, the ponderous nonsense perpetrated under the name of Nkrumaism did not fill the vacuum left by the colonial administration. Every country in the world has its corruption and political cynicism, but in Nkrumaist Ghana the youth had, as the republic constitution stated, no other "fount of honor," no other source of inspiration than Kwame Nkrumah. Consequently, the long night of Nkrumaist rule left Ghanaian youth with little more than an impression that politics was a fraud and a sham.

Constitutionality, as is true of all other legal terms, is not without ambiguity, allowing for divergent interpretation. However, Nkrumah's rise and, in particular, his seizure of power following independence can hardly be described as constitutional changes. The so-called referendums of 1960 and 1964, although nominally in accord with the constitution, were, in effect, coups against the people of Ghana. Nkrumah had raised unconstitutionality or extraconstitutionality to the level of an art, with the skillful assistance of Geoffrey Bing. In time, this particular feature of personal rule was to be interpreted by army and police officers as an authorization to disregard Nkrumah's constitution as well.

Again, it should be underlined that the argument here is not that Nkrumah failed because he subverted and abandoned the imperfect, perhaps irrelevant British institutions and practices.

His principal failure in institution-building was his refusal or inability to devise and to support alternatives. As a teacher of government and politics, which he fancied himself to be, he failed the youth of Ghana.

ECONOMIC DEVELOPMENT

There is no universal agreement on the meaning of development and progress, hence there is no agreement on what constitutes setbacks or failure in a development program. There simply are no universally valid criteria for measuring success.[14] However, one can assess a given social- and economic-development program against the yardstick of its own claims and targets.

Nkrumah certainly sketched and outlined, over the years, a panorama of development that can serve as a measure for evaluating the effect of personal rule on the country he led. Among the principal ingredients of the kind of program he envisaged were steady economic growth, fuller employment, increased per-capita income as well as a more equitably distributed income, and the provision of better housing. The basically one-crop economy was to be diversified and industrialization was to broaden and strengthen the base of the economy in general. Control over the economy was to be Africanized and vested in the state—i.e., in the people. The country was to be modernized, and living standards were to be improved markedly from year to year.

However, an evaluation of Nkrumah's rule, even by his own standards, is rendered problematic because of his devotion to the rather far-fetched foreign-policy goal of creating an all-Africa union government within the shortest possible time. Above all, there was the goal of transforming first Ghana, then the rest of Africa, into a socialist society—a goal that seems completely unrealistic in the light of any assessment of continental resources and capabilities. To measure the success or failure of Nkrumah's economic policies in Ghana in terms of the distance covered toward these shadowy goals would be futile indeed.

Yet, like Stalin, Nkrumah cannot be denied some credit for

achievement. When he left the Ghanaian scene as ruler, the landscape of Ghana was dotted with an impressive array of "monuments" to his vision, personal drive, initiative, and ambition, and to his dedication to the cause of liberating Africa from the shackles of colonialism. Unfortunately, there also stood the monuments to his frivolity and lack of sound judgment, to his overbearing arrogance, and to his vanity, false pride, and social injustice.

By general consensus, the principal monument to Nkrumah's drive, energy, and vision is the Volta River project at Akosombo, with its diverse and far-reaching benefits—its production of hydroelectric power and its potential for creating further industrialization, new sources of internal commerce, and new means of internal transportation. The project could eventually free millions of Ghanaians from the bonds of poverty and ignorance.[15]

The availability of relatively cheap sources of power (and there is some room for debate concerning the actual, as against projected, cost of the power produced at Akosombo) opened up truly formidable possibilities: the irrigation of the Accra plain, development of industry and agriculture up and down the west coast of Africa, and a general rise in living standards in Ghana. There stood the new port at Tema, locale of several dozen new industries, made accessible by new broad-lane highways. An entire industrial complex had been created in an attempt to wrest control of Ghana's economy from overseas suppliers. It was designed especially in order to permit Ghana to process her own natural resources, such as cocoa, bauxite, and timber, and to reduce her dependence on imports. Gold and diamond mining had been improved, oil prospecting was being pushed, and fifty-two or more government-owned and mixed-ownership enterprises had been created that were said to facilitate the African continent's most ambitious program of economic and social development.

On the strength of sheer numbers—of enterprises created or in process of construction, money spent by government on pupils

and students in schools and colleges, hospital beds, miles of new
road, pieces of mail transmitted, telephones and telephone lines
installed, newspapers circulated—the achievements were most impressive.[16]

TABLE 1

EDUCATIONAL STATISTICS, 1930–66

Year	Primary and Middle Schools		Secondary Government-Approved Schools		Teacher-Training Colleges	
	Number	*Total enrollment*	*Number*	*Total enrollment*	*Number*	*Total enrollment*
1930	340	41,917	4	538	7	555
1940	467	61,832	5	1,199	6	582
1950	1,592	204,262	12	2,776	19	1,831
1957	4,312	571,580	38	9,860	30	3,873
1958	....	580,366	39	10,400	..	4,055
1960	....	....	59	11,000-14,000*	39	....
1962	....	....	...	16,000*	..	....
1966	10,388	1,480,000*	101	35,000*	80	12,720*

SOURCES: H. O. A. McWilliam, *The Development of Education in
Ghana* (London: Longmans, Green, 1959), pp. 106, 107; *Directory of
the Republic of Ghana*, 1960, p. 18; Philip J. Foster, *Education and
Social Change in Ghana* (London: Routledge and Kegan Paul, 1965),
Tables 9, 10, 12; Nkrumah, *Parliamentary Debates, Official Record,*
February 1, 1966, cols. 11–12.

* Estimates.

The achievements would have seemed impressive to an observer who had last been in Ghana, say, in 1951, However,
what was most relevant was not so much what had been accomplished but what could have been accomplished, considering
Ghana's potential in human and material resources.

The Nkrumah years saw the gradual disappearance of the substantial reserve fund, which, at the time of independence, had amounted to some £200 million, and its replacement with a national debt of £349.2 million—fifteen times the size of the debt five years earlier.[17] The balance of payments had deteriorated to the point where the ambitious industrialization program was grinding to a halt. Export and import trade had been thrown into a state of chaos, foreign exchange had been depleted, and spare parts and raw materials were not available to operate many of the newly created state enterprises.[18] Taxation had almost reached the limit to which it could be extended. Civil service salaries had not been reviewed for nine years. The cost of living had risen so sharply—30 per cent higher in 1965 than a year earlier—that even Nkrumah had to admit it publicly. Wage-earners found it increasingly difficult to feed their families. The situation of the unemployed was becoming desperate. Robbery was on the increase and was becoming ever more brazen.[19]

The deterioration in these critical sectors of the economy tended to cancel out the benefits accruing from the relatively (by African standards) high wages and the embryonic social-security program. With a situation where hospitals were without drugs and vital equipment, where trucks were without tires and had to get along with makeshift repairs, it is likely that Nkrumah's declarations of substantial over-all progress, of the coming socialist paradise, became increasingly provocative and irritating to the Ghanaian public.

According to the last *Economic Survey* issued by the Ghanaian government before Nkrumah's removal, some of the more critical flaws in a fundamentally viable economic structure were: uneven growth—i.e., sharp relapses following forward spurts; external reserves lagging behind minimum import requirements needed to keep the economy producing; and a widening gap between the productivity of the constructed and projected physical and social infrastructure and the cost of loan repayments and service obligations. Short-term supplier credits were contracted to finance long-term delayed-profit development projects. All this drove up the national debt.

TABLE 2

REAL ECONOMIC GROWTH

(In Per Cents)

Year	
1960	7.5
1961	3.2
1962	5.3
1963	2.7
1964	4.5

SOURCE: *Economic Survey, 1964* (Accra, Government Printer), p. 15

A sympathetic interpretation of the chronic shortage of foreign exchange, the spiraling national debt, the shortages of essential and economically critical goods would see all this as the price needed to pay for liberating a former colony from the economic restraints imposed by "imperialism" and for correcting the economic imbalances and consequent social injustices that were part of the colonial legacy. A basic flaw in this line of reasoning is that it assumes that the post-independence regime sought and applied the best possible solutions. However, personal rule does not seem to be so oriented. For example, Nkrumah's industrialization policy, very much his own preserve and responsibility, was based on almost unbelievable miscalculations. On that count alone, it was not surprising that the growth rate could not steady itself.[20]

What we referred to earlier as the learning capacity of the political and social system—i.e., the capacity to accumulate and to improve knowledge and skills so as to assure the best possible use of resources—had been substantially diminished through personal rule. The demoralization and temporary de-intellectualization of Ghana's intelligentsia, the isolation of Ghana's youth from the mainsprings of twentieth-century thought under a regime of intellectual protectionism had deprived Ghana, and the social revolution in Africa, of its most critical resource—brain power.

A root cause of Ghana's economic woes was, very simply, the fact that the ruler insisted on being an economic czar without possessing the requisite technical skills, know-how, and sophistication. It was one thing to accuse the civil servants and both foreign and Ghanaian businessmen of failure to appreciate what was needed in a postcolonial, revolutionary society; it was quite another thing to find an adequate substitute for their insight and knowledge. Nkrumah was a man who displayed disdain for plans and planning; ordered grandiose projects; regarded accounting and accounting procedures as pettifoggery, as bourgeois relics; invited foreign capital yet repeatedly accompanied his invitations with eloquent denunciations of capitalism in all of its forms—investment, aid, and assistance. *Neo-Colonialism: The Last Stage of Imperialism*, proudly claimed by Nkrumah to be his contribution to "scientific socialism," was, significantly enough, written primarily by people who stood to lose very little, if anything, if the flow of investment to Ghana dried up—which is precisely what did happen, and much to the nation's detriment.

Consequently, fundamental mistakes were made which may not appear as such to victims of the euphoria that Nkrumah sought to propagate, but which were fully recognized by potential investors. The most serious error was the gross economic overextension, in terms of resources available, of markets, and of the world economic situation generally. In plain, hard economic terms, the right to a larger share of the world's wealth—which most African political leaders claim, and rightfully so—cannot be offered as collateral for loans or credits.

What made the situation worse, perhaps hopeless, was the possibility that the economy was being overextended in the wrong direction. The industrial projects selected by Nkrumah promised little in the way of returns for the country on the basis of the supply, trade, and finance patterns then prevailing. Too many of the Nkrumah-promoted projects threatened to become white elephants—in particular, the steel plant, the textile industry, the cocoa-processing plant, and the meat-processing plant.[21]

Once the development targets had been set out of reach of the available and potential resources, the restraints practiced under personal rule precluded the possibility of any real analysis being undertaken of the claim that the targets represented irreducible minimums. It was not possible to question the targets because the ruler had declared himself infallible; neither was it safe to question the assertion that the rest of the world had to adjust to the pace that Nkrumah had arbitrarily set for Ghana's development.

Whenever inquiries by outsiders became too embarrassing, the old standby charges of colonialist shortcomings and neocolonialist cunning were trotted out to divert attention from mismanagement at home.

Of course, the steady drop in the world price of cocoa contributed to Ghana's over-all economic weakness. Considering the heavy dependence on the sale of cocoa—about 60 per cent of all export trade—the drop from £467 per long ton in 1953 to £191 per long ton in 1963 was critical indeed. However, to insist, as Nkrumah did, that the Ghanaian economy was deteriorating simply because the consumers of the world's cocoa refused to pay higher prices was something of an exaggeration.[22] The overextension and mismanagement, the erratic course of Ghana's industrialization, the fanciful fiscal policies, and the misappropriations could not be ascribed to the consumers of Ghana's cocoa.

Personal mismanagement of Ghana's resources was the major cause for the repeated rejection of Ghana's requests for economic aid from outside sources, including the International Monetary Fund.[23] Although Nkrumah would not admit his guilt, when confronted with hard facts supplied by the International Monetary Fund, he retreated just a trifle; for a brief moment, he departed from the line that outside "imperialist and neocolonialist" forces alone were responsible for Ghana's problems and conceded, early in 1965 when an IMF mission was touring the country, that Ghana's "greatest single problem [was] that of economic administration."[24]

Even if one accepts Nkrumah's claim that the low world price of cocoa was the result of deliberate manipulation by "neocolonialist" interests intent on strangling independent African states— Ghana, of course, being the real target—one must still pose the question as to why drastic defense measures were not taken, why retrenchment, for instance, was not instituted when the economy revealed its first serious cracks. The reasons are self-evident. The economic retrenchment required would have triggered reactions leading to a more diligent and more persistent inquiry into Ghana's ills than Nkrumah's pseudo investigating commissions were prepared to conduct.[25] The search for the real causes would inevitably lead to the discovery of the central deficiency—Nkrumah himself.

Thus, at the end of the Nkrumah regime, the mass of the membership in all major socio-economic interest groups in the country—so readily designated as the "one-party" (state) by some academicians and the "socialist movement" by others—had probably ceased to identify themselves with the system. The rank and file of all groups had probably moved into opposition, a fact concealed from general view by the regimen of silence imposed upon the country by personal rule, and concealed from Nkrumah himself by the screen of flatterers, sycophants, and amateur samplers of public opinion with whom he had surrounded himself. While the adherents of the personal political machine were still sharing in the distribution of the cream that Nkrumah continued to skim off the top of the economy, the farmers, workers, public servants and, most crucial of all, the ranks and officers in the police and armed forces were gradually driven to the wall in terms of their earning and purchasing capacity. Economically, the country had reached rock bottom; the "one-party" bubble was about to burst.[26]

Considering the inability of all undeveloped countries to overcome, on their own, the handicap of a late start and to close the development gap, skillful conduct of foreign economic policies is one of the more critical responsibilities of such a government. Many of Nkrumah's difficulties stemmed from his inability or unwillingness to devise a reasonable, realistic, hence effective defense against what he termed "neocolonialism," a defense that would leave Ghana economically viable yet politically independent. Ill-advised, unable to brush aside the cobwebs of anachronistic Marxist cant and pseudo science, he devised a foreign policy that was harmful in terms of Ghana's economic interests. Instead of devising a foreign-policy formula that would permit some controlled bargaining with eager and willing Western business interests, he steered the economy of Ghana into a position where eventually all bargaining power was lost. Having maneuvered the Ghanaian economy into a position where official and reputable private sources of credit and "soft" loans were no longer available in sufficient volume to sustain his spending program, Nkrumah was forced to resort to unscrupulous marginal financiers—unscrupulous, that is, in their handling of their obligations toward Ghana; apparently profitable, however, to Nkrumah personally. Or he could have turned to the very tough negotiators from the far from charitable Communist states.

Appropriately, the end came while Nkrumah was on a diplomatic mission as self-styled arbiter of world affairs. In pursuit of spurious foreign-policy goals, he had tied the human and material resources of Ghana to his revolutionary chariot. Unable or unwilling to look back over his shoulder, he was dragging the economy and the people of Ghana into the dust.

IDEOLOGICAL, MORAL, AND AESTHETIC LEADERSHIP

Ideology

It is a near impossibility to fashion an ideology from a welter of confused, contradictory, haphazardly selected propositions. The neatly ordered and edited academic compilations on socialism in Africa and related topics reflect very little of the practical problems confronting ideologists in that setting today. The intellectual, social, and sociopsychological conditions prevailing during the fifteen years of Nkrumah's political rule simply were not favorable for the development or application of a socially relevant ideological framework, despite all the assertions to the contrary by his ardent advisers and collaborators from the four corners of the world.

Yet Nkrumah wants to be judged as an intellectual giant on the order of a Jefferson, a Sun Yat-sen, or a Lenin; some of the intellectuals rallying to his support shortly after the coup certainly appeared to see him in that light.[27] A summary evaluation of his ideological leadership is therefore in order.

The ideological function of political leadership is primarily to formulate and articulate guidelines for political and social behavior and to translate these into concrete plans and goals for state and society. To be reasonably effective, to release popular energies and direct them toward specific social objectives, the ideas must be manageable in practice, must be articulate, consistent, and socially relevant, and must be perceived by the opinion and action leaders throughout the state in approximately the sense intended.[28] To become and to remain socially relevant, the ideas must be subjected to wide-ranging and continuous discussion and review. To be of any practical use at all, the discussions and reviews must be conducted not only among the articulators—i.e., those persons with a vested interest in the acceptance of the ideas—but among disinterested observers employing objective methods of analysis and evaluation.[29]

Nkrumah's policy in this regard produced a number of sociopsychological conflicts that, unknown to him, rendered his entire ideological program inoperative from its very inception. For example, his reliance on the Russians (the Poles, Czechs, Hungarians, and East Germans were more flexible) highlighted the nearly unbridgeable gap separating the requirements of a newly emergent state from the doctrinaire goals of a thoroughly ideologized and settled society. As is the inevitable tendency of missionaries, the Russians were seeking to apply pure theory, while some of the less zealous, more pragmatic because more skeptical East Europeans and all of the African would-be Marxists were seeking to adjust the theory to fit the circumstances.

Although the entire activity amounted to little more than a storm in a teacup, confined largely to the faculty of the Ideological Institute at Winneba and to columns in *The Spark* and *The Ghanaian Times*, the resultant pontifical disputes deterred the emergence of a social theory of practical value to the development of Ghana. Thus was frustrated the very aim pursued by Nkrumah, the creation of an ideology relevant to Africa's needs. In his ideological kitchen, Nkrumah not only employed too many cooks of too many divergent backgrounds, but also failed to settle on the principal ingredients to be used.

The extraordinarily heavy reliance on extraneous foreign counsel was bad enough. Another root cause of the ideological failure was the likelihood that under personal rule, all ideas, good or bad, soundly conceived or naïve, are filtered through only one mind before gaining political acceptability. If that mind has definite limitations, as Nkrumah's has, the level of ideological activity can be devastatingly low.

Even if Nkrumah were the master political theorist that some of his foreign advisers and his admirers claimed he was, the exigencies of personal rule operated inexorably to restrict the flow of ideological activity to a trickle. Everything of substance was measured against the security requirements of the political machine.

Permissiveness with regard to fundamentally new ideas, although not necessarily leading to the collapse of the state, may well demonstrate the dispensability of the ruler. Furthermore, there is the clash between the principle of the Leader's infallibility and the requirements of intellectual growth. Where the ruler lacks the ability to perceive correctly the social and economic dimensions and the consequences of his ideological propositions, the country is, under personal rule, condemned to pursue the set course to the bitter end, or rebel. While the regime lasts, there is no effective way in which a basic ideological aberration or miscalculation can be corrected.

One of the most fantastic aspects of ideological activity under Nkrumah's rule and a major cause of his ultimate downfall was his totally false perception of the interests and aspirations of the people of Ghana. Unwilling to accept discouraging advice, fed platitudinous, wholly unfounded and untested generalizations by biased informants, Nkrumah built an elaborate ideological structure, albeit a rickety and socially irrelevant one, for the benefit of a hypothetical audience. His ideological pronouncements were directed at a public that his flattering, overenthusiastic functionaries and admirers assured him existed and that appeared to have substance at staged rallies and in the steady stream of inspired public and private protestations of loyalty but that in reality was a grand illusion.

A deficiency of catastrophic consequences for Ghana was Nkrumah's perception of the East-West conflict. Given to vast oversimplifications and to mistaking for eternal verities the personally flattering remarks disseminated by Moscow and Peking propagandists, he gravitated into a world where all evil resided on one side and all good on the other. It was a strange world of spies, assassins, and saboteurs, of continental, even world-wide conspiracies, emanating mainly from the United States, never from the Communist powers. The ample evidence of weakness in Western foreign-policy conduct that was presented to the world in the open, competitive press of the United States and Great Britain and in Western literature was eagerly seized upon by Nkrumah and his advisers to confirm their worst suspicions or designs. A book published in the United States on the Central Intelligence Agency was distributed at Nkrumah's personal direction to all government offices. Criticism of U.S. foreign policy advanced by a U.S. Senator on the floor of the Senate was accepted as confirmation of his theses, a speech to the contrary either ignored or written off as imperialist double talk or whitewash.

But the unavailability from the Communist camp of press reports, literature, or political pronouncements critical of Communism and Soviet or Chinese domestic or foreign policies was accepted by Nkrumah as evidence of Communism's great virtue and infallibility. For Nkrumah, the West could do very little right, and the East could do no wrong.

The tragedy for Ghana was that under personal rule, Nkrumah's bizarre perceptions were elevated to official doctrines, and state and society were irretrievably committed to disastrous policies. The foreign-trade follies, referred to above, in direct conflict with Ghana's vital interests, were cut from Kwame Nkrumah's ideological cloth.

At times this situation reached truly astonishing dimensions. In the spring of 1965, when a Ghanaian request for aid was lying on the desk of the American Ambassador to Ghana, Nkrumah personally authorized a demonstration against the U.S. Information Service and the Embassy. At about the same time, he cancelled an address by the U.S. Ambassador, while permitting in his personally controlled press a constant barrage of ideological assaults on the United States, including direct attacks on the foreign policy of its President. A few months later, while another aid request was being presented to the U.S. Government by a special delegation to Washington, his *Neo-Colonialism: The Last Stage of Imperialism* was being published. The book contained attacks on the Peace Corps and on the aid and assistance policies of the United States, including those of President Kennedy—who had removed the last blocks to United States participation in the Volta project. Granted that he had not written the book, U.S. authorities assumed nevertheless that the views expressed were his own. Consequently, the weak attempts by Nkrumah personally, his diplomatic representatives, and other spokesmen to explain away this apparent contradiction—he was asking for more, not fewer, Peace Corps missions and for more, not fewer, acts of economic assistance—were rejected. The Western governments did not go along with his strenuous efforts to disassociate his immediate responsibility to the Ghanaian people from his continental ideological adventures.[30]

All that the people of Ghana realized from Nkrumah's quaint interpretation of history was the painful experience of economic collapse. No progress was made toward the avowed revolutionary objectives that could not have been made more expeditiously and less painfully by other, more realistic, more astutely selected routes. Ghana was too small, too weak a country to be committed to the make-believe world of one misguided person.

There is no proof to support the contention that the painful experiences of the people of Ghana are worth-while sacrifices for the liberation of Africa—a proposition that should, of course, have been submitted to the people in a free and secret election and in clearly understandable, concrete terms. The requirements for the liberation of the continent have been and will remain subject to widely divergent interpretations among the people, among their rulers, and among the members of the Organization of African Unity. Nkrumah never did receive a mandate to interpret the requirements for all of Africa. Moreover, he arbitrarily sought to give the liberation of Africa a political orientation that would have made it a mere instrumentality of disputes and conflicts not necessarily of Africa's concern. His contention that his formula had been developed by "scientific socialism" was nonsense. There was in Nkrumah's perception of world affairs not one shred of truly scientific method.

One measure of the value of Nkrumah's contribution to ideological advancement in Ghana and in Africa generally is provided by the output of the pitiful project called the Kwame Nkrumah Ideological Institute at Winneba. This he had intended as the central academy for training revolutionary ideologists to further the Nkrumaist program for Ghana and for all of Africa. The situation at Winneba bordered on comedy. Assembled there were political theorists from the Soviet Union, Poland, and Czechoslovakia, very few of whom could make themselves understood in English. To these were added an odd mixture of political refugees, including the very able Sam Ikoku and Bankole Akpata. Also members of the staff were the all-purpose Professor Abraham and Dr. Ekow Daniels, prominent exponents of Nkrumaism.

The "students" at Winneba included traditional chiefs, youngsters with only the barest minimum of formal schooling, experienced "freedom fighters" from a variety of African countries and colonies, and an occasional party or government functionary enjoying a vacation from the cares of office while trying to make some sense of the cacophony of conflicting presentations. "Examinations" were uniformly administered to all, regardless of background, training, or ability.

The crowning achievement of the Institute was the production of a formula expressing the essence of Nkrumaism. This epoch-making event was described by one of the senior lecturers on the staff who had defected to London:

> No one really knew what Nkrumaism was, not even—I strongly suspected—the professional exegeists. After many months of intensive discussions, the Institute finally came up with an official definition that was approved by the Leader himself:
>
> "Nkrumaism is the ideology of the New Africa, independent and absolutely free from imperialism, organised on a continental scale, founded upon the conception of [a] one and united Africa drawing its strength from modern science and technology, and from the traditional African belief that the free development of each is the condition for the free development of all."
>
> What this meant no one could understand but all agreed that it was the true messianic revelation.[31]

In Africa, what is needed in the sphere of ideological synthesis, aside from the political decisions that must be made by Africans themselves, is collation, interpretation, and application of the best, most cogent, most relevant ideas advanced in the rest of the world and by teams of scholars, educators, and practical communications specialists. Personal rule in Ghana thwarted such

an effort. As a result, the first attempt to evolve an African answer to Socialism, Marxism, Communism, and the social-revolutionary requirements of Ghana and of the continent turned into
a grotesque attempt to graft onto the body of Africa wholly
unrelated fragments from Stalin's Russia, Hitler's Germany, from
Marcus Garvey, Malcolm X, and Lenin.

Nkrumaism was not an ideology. It was an indigestible brew
concocted by a cynical assembly of mercenaries, "hit-and-run"
experts, sincere but frustrated political theorists, and charlatans.

In *Consciencism,* Lenin's dictum is cited: "Practice without
thought is blind: thought without practice is empty."[32] In Nkrumaist Ghana, practice was controlled by irrational thought and
articulated largely by mediocrities. Propagandistically, Nkrumah
had succeeded in numbing the collective mind of Ghana by promoting a cacophony of ideological double talk and Byzantine
cant. He had also succeeded in projecting a favorable image
among a substantial portion of the less-informed, because more
distant, frustrated youth elsewhere in Africa. This was especially
true of students in African countries whose governments were
taking a less radical, less revolutionary stance than Nkrumah.
Ideologically, he had only succeeded in making an articulate and
able people temporarily deaf and dumb and in confusing the
issues confronting Africa in general.

Moral and Aesthetic Leadership

No basis exists for criticizing moral and aesthetic leadership
in a developing country unless a claim for success is made. And
the developing countries should be entitled to their period of
trial.

However, Nkrumah and his rule cannot be spared criticism.
Nkrumah and his disciples claimed that he was, with minor
lapses, a paragon of virtue, a symbol of morality, propriety, and
high aesthetic judgment. Because the facts about his rule are
rapidly turning into legend and what is remembered of the man

may be turned into a total myth in the minds of his devotees, it is vitally important that the claims be subjected to close analysis while memories are fresh.

Nkrumah apparently took seriously his self-appointed role as "Fount of Honor." However, his contributions on moral and aesthetic matters were confined to prescriptions and propaganda; practice was quite another matter.

His most celebrated effort to reverse the trend toward moral disintegration was the famous "Dawn Broadcast." But the salient fact was that most of his admonitions were manifestations of wishful thinking, were practically unrealizable, and, most important, were not going to be followed by Nkrumah himself. Nkrumah's unwillingness to follow his own prescriptions was one of his basic deficiencies. This was glibly ignored by his protagonists, who, acknowledging that the leadership of Nkrumaist Ghana was not the best possible, ascribed this shortcoming to his reluctance to take drastic measures, to "make heads roll." Nor did they admit to his total lack of humility and his commitment to rather sordid tactics simply to stay in power.[33] The underlying cause of the moral failure, and of the related aesthetic one as well, was again the limitation imposed upon a nation by personal rule.

Year after year, expressions of mirth greeted his demands that others repatriate capital holdings spirited out of the country and hidden in bank accounts abroad. Ministers and backbenchers laughed when he raised the issue in the National Assembly, for it was common knowledge that Nkrumah himself was one of the largest holders of hidden foreign assets[34]—despite the posture of national dedication and personal austerity that he preached. As has been pointed out already, these holdings consisted substantially of misappropriated funds that had been skimmed off government contracts. Evidence came to light after the coup indicating that part of these funds were used to subvert Ghana. Some of his personal wealth—invested in a gambling casino, numerous palaces, and various enterprises at home and abroad—was also banked in Ghana. Preaching socialism, Nkrumah was one of the country's most active and successful capitalists, operating an insurance firm with captive clientele and investing his misappropriated funds in capitalist enterprises in the "imperialist" world. It was not a surprise to his Commissioner of Police when Nkrumah, upon being informed of spreading bribery and corruption in highest government and party circles, time and again turned down requests for punitive, corrective action.[35]

The construction of luxurious villas and palatial official residences, the bestowal of expensive gifts upon favorites, including female friends, despite statutory provisions governing the use of public funds, the most conspicuous consumption and lavish entertainment wholly out of line with prevailing conditions, and his lack of discretion in his private affairs—all served to make Nkrumah an unlikely symbol of morality or source of moral inspiration.[36]

Yet, under his rule, there was no alternative symbol or source of inspiration. In Nkrumaist Ghana, the Leader monopolized the positions and roles held in other societies by a variety of people and agencies: churches, philosophers and writers, historical and mythical figures. Even the function of Christ as a moral symbol had been pre-empted by the Osagyefo. Simultaneously, the assemblage of opportunists in the party and its auxiliary organizations had supplanted the social forces, voluntary and private, that could play a constructive role in these areas.

Although it deals with only one aspect of Nkrumah's failure to be a moral force, the following passage from the Parliamentary debates in August, 1965, is revealing. In a delightfully unguarded moment, one MP blurted out a basic problem of Nkrumaist Ghana:

> Osagyefo, the President, ended his address [to the Assembly] by calling upon the nation to rid itself of a disease. This disease must be removed from our society before Ghana can make any real progress. That disease is "G.R.Q." get-rich-quick. The first cause of this

disease is that some Ghanaians are ostentatious. Every young man wants to live like Osagyefo. [A Member: "It is a good aspiration."] That is a wrong aspiration; it is overambition.[37]

Nation-building, moving a country like Ghana into the twentieth century, is a most difficult assignment. It is more difficult and more challenging than similar tasks performed centuries ago by political and spiritual leaders in the more advanced parts of the world. It is too big a task for any one man. That he attempted it virtually singlehandedly was perhaps Nkrumah's major failing, for it reduced Ghana's chances of survival by the measure of his inability.

Nkrumah had lost contact with the spiritual achievements of mankind, the arts, the more lasting values of human existence. Intrigued by the potentialities of politics, he had become bogged down in the grubby, workaday pursuits of machine-building, in a perpetual, ever more intense struggle for political survival. He had not allowed himself the luxury of developing his mind, expanding his interests, and refining his enjoyments. That had been his choice and his privilege. Unfortunately for the 7 million Ghanaians, his choice became the enforced standard of behavior for all. Nkrumah's limited tastes in theater and the arts, in architecture and literature were imposed upon a virile and vibrant people, thereby drying up the wellsprings of creative talent.

Much effort was expended in propagating the myth that the regime of mediocrity that Nkrumah sought to impress upon Ghana was of African heritage. It was nothing of the sort. Its origins, its sources of inspiration—glibly identified with Africa's past by some sleight of hand—were nowhere to be found on the continent of Africa. In the main, the world of Kwame Nkrumah and his followers was unreal, a world of youthful dreams gone astray, of ideals barely perceived but soon subverted and harnessed to cynical pursuit of power. It was a world in which the ghosts of Hitler and Stalin, of Fascism, Communism, and Marxism, were allowed to rise again and assume real-life proportions.

In the world of Nkrumah, there was no room for reasoned

debate, the application of liberal and humane reasoning to the whole range of government. There was only dedication to half-truths and emotional appeals and the effort to put those to work for the political machine.

In at least some respects, Nkrumah's style of rule warrants commendation. His march to power was accompanied by relatively little violence (excluding deaths incurred in partisan political skirmishes by all sides in the 1956 election campaign and thereafter and deaths and destruction accompanying the 1948 disturbances). In fact, the much celebrated "march" on Christianborg Castle in 1948, leading to the deaths of two ex-servicemen and the wounding of five innocent bystanders in a fusillade by an excited police sergeant, as compared with similar but far bloodier demonstrations elsewhere in the developing world, remains a symbol less of revolutionary heroism than of a relatively peaceful approach to the power struggle. More significant and remarkable in the light of massacres involving thousands of innocents in other African states, at no time does Nkrumah appear to have intentionally caused the death of a single person. From 1957, when he attained full executive power —setting aside the fiction of the constitutional monarchy still resorted to at that time—through 1965, apparently not one single political execution took place in Ghana. Whatever the reasons, he must be given credit for this. One cannot fail to concur with the view expressed by a source usually quite critical of his regime:

> It is a fact to be remembered when regretting the many steps that have been taken in Ghana away from the ideals embodied in her national motto "Freedom and Justice," that no single execution of a political opponent has been carried out, an example that should be reflected upon by political leaders facing internal dissent both in Africa and elsewhere.[38]

However, the numerous prisons in Ghana were unsanitary, even filthy, commitment carried with it a high probability of injury to the detainee's health, and Nkrumah was insensitive to reports of suffering among the prisoners he had personally ordered detained. Considering the arbitrary nature of detention as practiced under Nkrumah, he cannot be absolved entirely of responsibility for a number of deaths in detention and for the impaired state of health of many of the surviving detainees. Nor can he be absolved of responsibility for the suffering of the families. Since he had been apprised of the impaired health of his most distinguished prisoner, Dr. J. B. Danquah, by the latter's former wife, he must bear the responsibility for Dr. Danquah's death in prison on February 4, 1965.[39]

Epilogue

It would appear that one absolute requirement for maintaining personal rule is continuous physical presence of the ruler at the center of the control machinery. Since all major and critical decisions must be made by the ruler and only he knows his way through the maze of security arrangements and communication channels, a security breakdown can reasonably be expected if he is not at his post in an emergency.

Although the danger signs had been mounting steadily since the middle of 1965, Nkrumah had good reason not to fear significant action from civilian groups. And he was confident that any oppositional notions among the military would be brought to his attention in time to organize countermeasures.

Yet informed circles in Ghana had expected some kind of action by army units for some time. An attempted coup was rumored to have been staged as recently as January 19, 1966.[1] Everything considered, Nkrumah's decision to fly to Peking and Hanoi on February 21 in order to take a personal hand in negotiations concerning the war in Viet-Nam was nothing short of amazing. It was most doubtful that the presence in Hanoi of the President of Ghana would in any significant way have altered the attitudes of the major world powers locked in that struggle. Nkrumah's decision to leave the country at that time on a mission of such dubious value may constitute the ultimate proof that he had become detached from reality.

When army brigades—possibly numbering only 600 men—supported by the police and its Criminal Investigation Department struck in the early morning hours of February 24, 1966, the vaunted "one-party state" evaporated almost without a trace. Even the political machine disintegrated quickly, with several of

171

its principal beneficiaries vying to be among the first to denounce the fallen idol. The Nkrumaists in the trade unions, the farmers' organization, the national and local bureaucracy, the Workers Brigade, in fact everywhere, quietly sought to lose themselves in the gathering crowd of jubilant supporters of the new regime.

Within hours after the coup, Nkrumah evidently lost whatever popular support he had held in the major cities of Accra, Kumasi, Cape Coast, Koforidua, and Secondi-Takoradi. He failed to inspire anyone outside the special forces at Flagstaff House to offer active resistance to the new revolutionary regime. The traditional structure, never much of a political force but deeply wounded by the political machine, quickly rallied to the support of the new regime.

As the people danced, demonstrated, and paraded in the streets, those in and outside Ghana whose sole source of information had been the machine-controlled propaganda mill were stunned at the apparent emptiness of the mass-mobilization society. Also incredulous were those whose assessment of Nkrumah's strength had been based primarily on sympathy or wishful thinking.

The reasons for the apparent mystery have now been set forth. In summary, Nkrumah's regime had been superimposed upon a politically inexperienced and, in essential respects, politically paralyzed and disoriented people. From 1951 on, first as Leader of Government Business and later as Prime Minister, Nkrumah was the principal Ghanaian wielder of coercive controls. Subject to over-all but sympathetic supervision by the colonial administration, he had had at his disposal army units stationed in Ghana (then the Gold Coast), the police, and the Criminal Investigation Department, as well as additional means of coercion. In short, from the beginning, he enjoyed a virtual monopoly of the power held by Ghanaian leaders in an essentially nonresistant, nonpolitical environment. Personal rule seemed so successful largely because it had been installed in a political vacuum. What opposition there had been, mainly in Ashanti and in enclaves along the coast, including sections of Accra, had been relatively easily isolated, surrounded, divided, and cut down.

Personal rule in Ghana had been able to sustain itself for so long because it had been the sole, unchallenged repository of power, influence, and coercion in Ghana until the morning of February 24, 1966; but neither Nkrumah nor his machine had ever struck roots in the soil of Ghana. The Nkrumaist regime had been conceived not merely as an answer to the social, economic, and political problems of Ghana but as a device of far wider scope, as an instrument of a world-wide political revolutionary movement, hazily perceived by Nkrumah and his aides as "anti-imperialist, anti-colonialist, anti-neocolonialist." In a way, Nkrumah had hijacked Ghana's administration, economy, army, police force, and political platform for purposes substantially unrelated to the interests and aspirations of the majority of Ghanaians. Under the false flags of freedom, justice, and socialism, supported by a cabal of foreign advisers whose vision did not encompass the needs of Ghana—or of Africa for that matter—Nkrumah had insinuated himself into the hearts of a segment of an unsuspecting people. He had told them that they should first "take the political kingdom and all other things would be added." Gradually, it had become apparent that by "all other things" Nkrumah had not meant freedom, material well-being, and real progress for Ghanaians. Instead, he had committed the future of Ghana to the pursuit of extraneous political goals.

The Achilles' heel of personal rule in Ghana, as in so many other countries, had been the alienation of the regime from the masses. The sudden collapse of the façade revealed the cold, ruthless, cynical, impersonal nature of personal rule. When the central controlling figure that had held the artificial structure together was out of the country and when the monopoly of coercive power was challenged by the army brigades, the overwhelming unpopularity of Nkrumah's rule was exposed.

The political machine itself lacked resilience. There was no firm organizational framework; the only generally known fact was that there was a center. The component parts of the machine could act only through the center; direct communication was discouraged. Communication within the machine was furtive, conspiratorial, spiteful.

The machine generated no real loyalty; what little there was was the product of intimidation, even terror, or the precarious fellowship laced with mutual contempt of accomplices in crime.

Ideologically, the machine hung suspended between irreconcilable poles: personal aggrandizement and universal political and social conflict. There was a rhetorical identification with the vague, amorphous longings of Africa's masses, and countering that, a surrender to graft, bribery, and corruption. The goal of Africa's liberation was obscured, in the vision of Nkrumah and his supporters, by the goal of self-gratification. For the colonial mentality, which it avowedly detested, the regime substituted the machine mentality: The court philosophers and machine scribes were no more accurate or faithful to history than the sources they attacked; talking scientific socialism, they subscribed to a regime that by its very nature dreaded scientific analysis.

Even without the military coup, the machine stood in danger of internal collapse from decay induced by its inner contradictions.

There is sufficient evidence that Nkrumah had begun to sense his loss of popularity. In the face of spreading hostility, of dissension in the machine, party, trade unions, and elsewhere, he canceled the election of June, 1965. Almost desperately, he strove to strengthen his defenses, primarily his private army, in order to ward off the expected blow. But evidently his estimate of the unpopularity of his rule was inadequate. In the end, his judgment proved to be fatally wrong.

A few weeks before the end, Nkrumah addressed the non-elected Parliament at the state opening. Seeking to explain the several military coups that had erupted across the continent, he made these unwittingly prescient observations on the theme of military action against corrupt regimes:

As we all know, within the last few months there have been un-
fortunate military intrusions into the political life of several independent African states. . . .

What therefore has led to the military intrusions and interference
and violence which we are now witnessing? Why is it that the armies
of certain African states have been forced to take the steps which
they have taken? We must examine critically and carefully the underlying forces and circumstances which have given rise to these up-
heavals. Their root cause can be found not in the life and tradition
of the African people, but in the maneuvers of neocolonialism.

Substitute "international opportunism" or "pseudosocialism"
for "neocolonialism," and the observations fit perfectly the fiasco
of personal rule in Ghana. Not realizing that but for a few words
he was describing the root cause of his own overthrow, which
would occur three weeks later, Nkrumah went on to say further:

> In a neocolonialist state, the leaders of the Government allow them-
> selves to be used and manipulated by foreign states and financial
> interests. The whole regime . . . is therefore subject to remote con-
> trol. In other words, the rulers and governors of the . . . regime are
> teleguided from afar. These foreign powers and interests seek to
> maintain the exploitation and oppression of the people even after
> independence. Corruption, bribery, nepotism, shameless and riotous
> and ostentatious living become rife among the leaders of the . . .
> regime. This brings untold suffering on the workers and people as a
> whole. The masses become lethargic and see no reason to make any
> sacrifices for their country.
>
> The masses have then nowhere to turn for redress. They therefore
> have no choice but to organise to isolate the army from the corrupt
> regime, if the army itself is free from the taint of corruption.[2]

The regimes Nkrumah described and his own differed in a
number of respects—e.g., in the degree to which foreign interests
predominated. However, they were strikingly similar in other respects. Whereas personal rule in Ghana was not puppet rule, it
was alien rule, nevertheless, and as such could not expect the
people to tolerate abuses any more than if it had been directly
controlled from abroad.

It appears that the rebellious army and police officers certainly questioned the legitimacy of Nkrumah's rule and the extent to which they owed him allegiance. Nkrumah had grossly miscalculated in this respect also. Like some of the Nigerian leaders whose faults he presumed to judge, he had regarded loyalty as a one-way street; everyone owed him unquestioned loyalty and obedience, but he remained free to interpret his oath of office as he saw fit. While officers, civil servants, and judges were bound to adhere rigidly to their traditional code of nonpolitical conduct, Nkrumah, under that convenient arrangement, was free to conspire with foreigners against the constitutional order he had sworn to uphold. He was free to rig elections, misappropriate funds, subvert Parliament, corrupt politics and politicians, lower the standards of leadership, and hire mercenaries to oppose the regular armed forces. He was free to do all this because his policies represented correct scientific socialism, anti-imperialism, anti-neocolonialism, Africanism.[3]

Loyalty has its limits. Nkrumah's failure to appreciate this was his final miscalculation. It had been one thing for the colonial government to import officers and military advisers. It was quite another for the liberator of Ghana and would-be liberator of all of Africa, sworn to uphold his country's newly-won independence, to turn the security responsibilities in Ghana over to a secret army, once again directed, trained, and supplied by non-Africans. To expect Ghanaian officers and men to accept the creation of an instrument designed to destroy them, and in a cause that had never been endorsed by the people and that was anathema to most elements in the army and the police, was expecting too much. Whatever additional grievances may have motivated the army and police officers, and there were several others, the turning over of security to foreigners was an unacceptable move.

A likely argument one can expect to hear advanced in defense of Nkrumah and his rule is that "he was a good man misled by bad advice."[4] Often after major disasters of the type that befell

Nkrumah and his supporters across the continent of Africa, a simple, plausible legend will be fostered analogous to the "stab-in-the-back" legend circulated by the German General Staff in 1918 to blame the civilian politicians for Germany's loss of World War I. Now it will be said that if it had not been for bad foreign advisers, Nkrumah would have finished the revolution he had begun. The legend will be broadened to blame the wicked military and police officers as well.

That there were foreign advisers, and that they played a role in the drama, is a point that has been made in this study. But the point has also been made that the abundance of bad advice was the direct consequence of Nkrumah's rejection of good advice. Beyond the personal failings of Kwame Nkrumah, the blame must be placed upon personal rule.

One student of Latin America, in an attempt to justify right-wing dictatorship there, asserted: "The basic issue is not whether the government is dictatorial or is representative and constitutional. The issue is whether the government, whatever its character, can hold the society together sufficiently to make the transition."[5] Is that *the basic* issue? Is it the basic issue in Africa?

If there were not other alternatives, one might have to resign oneself to accepting any dictatorship. But there are alternatives, a whole spectrum of alternatives developed by mankind over a period of 4,000 years. By allowing the political machine to forge chains to hold a society in transition together, one assists in creating a myth—the myth of the inevitability of dictatorship. Soon the "holding of the society together" turns into a personality cult that reduces the nation to a state of collective stupor, or even madness, leading it to ultimate disaster.

In the light of human experience, there is no convincing reason why the words of John F. Kennedy spoken with regard to Latin America cannot also be applied to Africa: "To complete the revolution of the Americas . . . political freedom must accompany material progress . . . *progreso si, tirania no!*"[6]

CHRONOLOGY OF MAJOR EVENTS IN NKRUMAH'S LIFE

1909   Born Kofi Nwiah Kwame Nkrumah September 21 (?) in the Nzima area of southwest Gold Coast.

1935   Enters Lincoln University, Pennsylvania.

1939   Graduates with B.A. Enters Lincoln Theological Seminary and University of Pennsylvania.

1942   Graduates with B.A. Theol., M.Sc. Phil., M.A. Phil.
–43

1945   Reads law at Gray's Inn, London. Attends lectures at London
–47   School of Economics. Joint Secretary (with George Padmore) of Fifth Pan-African Congress. General Secretary of West African National Secretariat.

1947   Founds "Circle." Returns to Gold Coast when invited to become General Secretary of the United Gold Coast Convention (UGCC). First purge of political associates.

1948   Disturbances in the Gold Coast. Major leaders of UGCC arrested. Nkrumah released to give evidence to Watson Commission.

1949   Founding of Convention People's Party (CPP) in June.

1950   "Positive Action," civil disobedience campaign, leads to imprisonment.

1951   Elected to Legislative Assembly (still in prison). Victory of CPP. Release from prison and appointment as Leader of Government Business. Formation of his first "cabinet."

1952   Becomes Prime Minister in March.

1954   Elections. Defections from CPP. Formation of National Liberation Movement.

1956   "Independence election." Internal strife. Jibowu inquiry.

1957   Independence, March 6. Disturbances among the Ga-Adangbe. Restrictions on opposition.

1958   First Conference of Independent African States, in Accra. Preventive Detention Act (PDA). Ghana-Guinea Union. Arrests of thirty-eight members of the opposition. Visit to United States; Volta River Project revived.

1959   George Padmore dies. "Second Revolution" proclaimed.

1960   Plebiscite and republic constitution, July 1. President with official title Osagyefo.

1961   Economy sagging. "Dawn Broadcast." Secretary General of CPP. Visit to U.S.S.R., China, Eastern Europe. Takoradi strike. Purge of conservatives (Gbedemah, Botsio, Edusei, etc). Censorship.

1962   Kulungugu attempt on his life. Welbeck, Botsio, Edusei reinstated. Adamafio and others purged. PDA extended. Bomb "outrages."

1963 Acquittal of Kulungugu group. Dismissal of Chief Justice. Stepped-up internal security measures.

1964 Flagstaff House attempt on his life. One-party referendum. Police purged.

1965 Pardons of Kulungugu group. Dismissal of army leaders.

1966 Volta River Project inaugurated in January. Departure for Hanoi via Peking on February 21. Coup, February 24.

APPENDIX II

THE GOVERNMENT OF GHANA[1]

February, 1966

A. The President (Constitutional, Statutory, and Derivative Powers)
   Supreme Command of Armed Forces
   Office of the President
      Special Services
         Presidential Guard, Secret Service, Foreign Intelligence, Border Control, Espionage, Counterespionage
      Commissions of Investigation
      Publicity Secretariat*
         Press, Radio, Television, NAPADO Enterprise (Advertising Distribution)
      Constitutional Affairs
      Traditional Councils, Houses of Chiefs*
      Architectural and Engineering Secretariat*
      State Control Commission
      Presidential Enterprises (National Development Company [NADECO], etc.)
   Auditor General's Department*
   Office of the Planning Commission*

[1] SOURCES: Ghana, *The Annual Estimates for 1965* (Part I: *The Consolidated Fund*), Vol. I: *The President* (also volumes on *Interior, Foreign Affairs, Defence*); *The Budget, 1965; Government Organisation Manual,* June, 1965; *Instrument of Incorporation of the State Enterprises,* L.I. No. 467 (1965); *Handbook on State Enterprises,* 1965.

* Special departments and divisions in which the President exercised ministerial responsibility.

National Productivity Center
National Planning Commission
  State Planning Commission
Water Resources and Power Secretariat
Volta River Authority
State Functions Secretariat*
Establishment Secretariat*
  Civil Service Commission
Central Bureau of Statistics*
African Affairs Secretariat
  Ghana diplomatic missions in Africa
  All-African Affairs, including Organization of African Unity, African interests in the United Nations and other international organizations
Regional organizations*
  Regional Commissioners
  Regional Party Organization and Propaganda
  Internal Security
  Local Authorities including District Commissioners
  Elections
  Tender Boards, Land Planning, and Acquisition
Organization and Methods Secretariat*
Higher Education and Research
  Secretariat For Higher Education
    National Council for Higher Education
    University of Ghana
    Kwame Nkrumah University of Science and Technology
    University College of Cape Coast
    School of Administration
    Institute of Statistics
    Institute of Public Education
    Kwame Nkrumah Ideological Institute
    Institute of African Studies
    Special Professorships
    General Legal Council
    Ghana Universities Press
    University of Ghana: Volta River Basin Research Program
    Institute of Chartered Accountants
  Scholarship Secretariat*
    All government scholarships, at home and overseas
    All government scholarships awarded to citizens of other African states
    All Ghana Cocoa Marketing Board scholarships
    All scholarships offered to Ghana by foreign governments, organizations, and international agencies

Commonwealth awards to students of other Commonwealth
countries
Ghana Academy of Sciences*
Atomic Energy Commission*
Scientific research in medicine, agriculture, etc.
Institute of Art and Culture
Cultural agreements with other countries
Promotion of art and culture throughout Ghana
State Enterprises Secretariat* (Nominal responsibility assigned to
ministers)
All state corporations, including:
Ghana National Trading Corporation
Ghana State Mining Corporation
Ghana Airways Corporation
Black Star Line
State Farms Corporation
Ghana National Construction Corporation
Ghana Aluminum Products
State Cocoa Marketing Board
State Tele-Communication Corporation
State Housing Corporation
State Diamond Marketing Corporation
Guinea Press
Local and Municipal Councils Secretariat
Grants-in-Aid
Local Government Service
Elections
Property Valuation
Office of the National Assembly
Office of the Chairman and Secretary General of the CPP
All Party Auxiliaries
Trade Union Congress
Workers Brigade
United Ghana Farmers' Council Cooperatives
National Council of Ghana Women
Young Pioneers
Bank of Ghana (and other state-owned or controlled banks)
The Courts
B. Cabinet and Noncabinet Departments†
Cabinet
Finance
Interior
Communications
Science and Education
Industries

Trade
Information and Broadcasting
Party Propaganda
Foreign Affairs
Justice
Works
Agriculture
State Planning Commission
Defence
Health
Noncabinet
Parks and Gardens
Animal Husbandry
Food and Nutrition
Local Government
Housing
Labour
Fuel and Power
Art and Culture
Lands
Pensions and National Insurance
Social Welfare
Mines and Mineral Resources
Fisheries
Rural Industries
Cooperatives

All critical ministerial functions had been transferred to the President's Office and the Secretariat—e.g., Armed Forces from Defence, Commerce from Trade, Banking and Foreign Exchange from Finance, Major Contracting from all departments, Police from Interior, Development Expenditures from all departments, Radio and Television from Information and Broadcasting, Higher Education and Research from Education. Most of the ministries and departments were hollow shells, at best clerical annexes to the presidency.

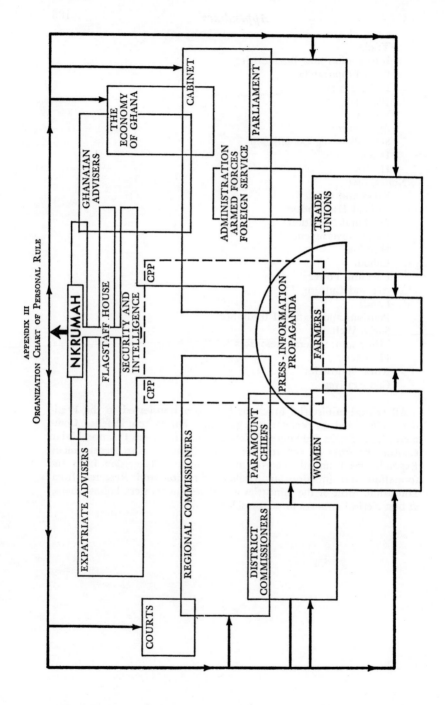

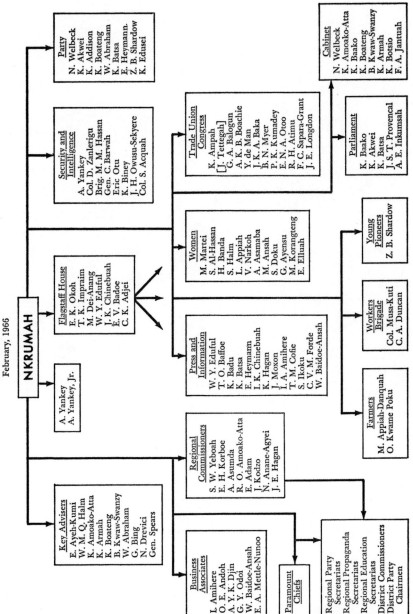

Notes*

PREFACE

1. See Bretton, "Current Political Thought and Practice in Ghana," *The American Political Science Review*, LII, No. 1 (March, 1958), 46–63.

INTRODUCTION

1. Bretton, *Power and Stability in Nigeria: The Politics of Decolonization* (New York: Frederick A. Praeger, 1962); "Power and Influence in Southern Nigeria," in Herbert J. Spiro (ed.), *The Primacy of Politics in Africa* (New York: Random House, 1966), pp. 49–84, 171–87.
2. My approach to the subject of this book was influenced to a considerable extent by Stanley D. Beck, *The Simplicity of Science* (Harmondsworth: Penguin Books, 1959); Norbert Wiener, *The Human Use of Human Beings* (New York: Anchor Books, 1954); Karl W. Deutsch, *The Nerves of Government: Models of Political Thought and Control* (New York: The Free Press of Glencoe, 1963); and David Easton, *A Framework for Political Analysis* (Englewood Cliffs, N.J.: Prentice-Hall, 1965).
3. See Ann Ruth Willner, "The Underdeveloped Study of Political Development," *World Politics*, XVI, No. 3 (April, 1946), 468–82.
4. Avoidance of discussion of the role of money in politics often is justified on the grounds that reliable documentation may not be available and that treatment of such matters would therefore be speculative. It seems to me that the same argument might apply to many profusely documented analyses.
5. Duverger, *Political Parties* (London: Methuen; New York: John Wiley & Sons, 1954), p. 147.

I. BACKGROUND TO PERSONAL RULE

1. Leonard W. Doob, *Communication in Africa: A Search for Boundaries* (New Haven, Conn.: Yale University Press, 1961),

---

* Acts of Parliament, statutory instruments, bills, and enactments of Constituent Assemblies, are not referenced beyond the official title. They can be located by date in the appropriate compilations—e.g., *Acts of Ghana* (Accra, Government Printer), *The Ghana Law Reports* (Accra, The General Legal Council), and *Ghana Gazette* (Accra, Government Printer).

treats of the basic difficulties in political communication and political participation that is almost wholly ignored by generalizers on nation-building, the mass party, etc. The problem was graphically illustrated by an MP in discussing the difficulties encountered by the government in attempting to communicate the essence of a budget to the people. He related the following incident: "A certain young man attended an interview and he was asked to explain what was meant by this: 'The Government of Nigeria has placed a ban on all South African goods because of their apartheid policy.' This was a simple sentence. When the man was asked to translate it into Fanti or Twi, he said: '*Nigeria Aban ato nsa afre South Africa Aban de wombobo baan wo Nigeria na yebobo pata ama woatsena ase.*' Meaning, literally, that the Government of Nigeria has invited the South African Government to come and play band in Nigeria and they will raise a shed for them to sit under." (J. K. Twum, *Parliamentary Debates, Official Report*s [hereafter cited as *Debates*], January 28, 1965, col. 450.) For a contrary (wholly impressionistic) view concerning public opinion and perceptions, see Thomas Hodgkin, "Relevance of 'Western' Ideas for African States," in J. Roland Pennock (ed.), *Self-Government in Modernizing Nations* (Englewood Cliffs, N.J.: Prentice-Hall, 1964), pp. 60–61. Hodgkin notes an awareness of "the great issues with which they are confronted," among "representatives of the masses with whom I have been personally acquainted," and finds that they "have usually had a pretty clear understanding of the concept of the sovereignty of the people." One is left to wonder by what methods of analysis Hodgkin reached his conclusions, with what sample of the masses he managed to become personally acquainted, and what degree of perception is meant by "pretty clear understanding." In my research, I found that much depends on how questions are formulated.

2. A recurring theme seeks to relate the functions of a modern government, of parliament, and of the courts to traditional institutions and practices. The superficial changes that were effected in the Ghanaian National Assembly were a case in point: The substitution of African for British parliamentary ritual had no bearing whatever on the purposes or functions of parliament.

3. Certain trappings associated with chieftaincy and used by Nkrumah in the earlier stages of his march to power were dropped later in favor of Soviet and Chinese totalitarian symbols and practices.

4. See Bretton, *Power and Stability in Nigeria*, Part I.

5. In the course of my first interview with Nkrumah, in August, 1956, when I mentioned that it had been suggested that perhaps

Ghana needed for a time what might be termed a "benevolent dictatorship," Nkrumah responded: "That is what the Governor says."

6. At independence, Ghana was the sixth largest producer of gold in the world and the fourth largest producer of manganese. On the average, the Gold Coast had contributed 25 per cent of the dollar earnings of all British colonial territories. During 1951–55, the Gold Coast contributed a net positive balance of £153 million, including her gold contributions, to the gold and dollar reserves of the sterling area.

7. *Ghana: The Autobiography of Kwame Nkrumah* (London and New York: Thomas Nelson, 1957), p. x; references to the close cooperation between the Governor and Nkrumah are found in *ibid.,* p. 282, and in F. M. Bourret, *Ghana: The Road to Independence, 1919–1957* (London: Oxford University Press, 1960), pp. 175, 177.

8. There were, of course, individual jurists, academicians, and writers in Britain who took a different position. I make reference here only to what might be termed the national interest, and that is usually not determined by legal or political theorists. Economic considerations weighed more heavily and favored the support of whoever promised political stability and the continuation of profitable trade relations with Great Britain. Under the prevailing conditions, Nkrumah was strongly favored. After the failure of the attempt to restrain him through the creation of five autonomous regions, London completely accepted Nkrumah. A glance at the trade balance over the years shows that the choice had actually not been a bad one from balance-of-trade considerations. See, for example, Ghana, *External Trade Statistics,* XV, No. 8 (August, 1965), xii–xiii. In fact, it appears that Nkrumah's opposition to "neocolonialist" practices did not apply to Great Britain to the same extent as it did to the United States.

9. Given the fact that institutional and procedural factors generally influence political behavior in a society, the extreme fluidity of the legal-constitutional framework in Ghana made discovery of regularities in public behavior extremely unlikely. Generalizations concerning legal value-judgments, legal norms, etc., would, under the circumstances, be quite meaningless. See Bretton, "Current Political Thought and Practice in Ghana," p. 46.

10. Nkrumah, *I Speak of Freedom* (New York: Frederick A. Praeger, 1961), pp. 72, 99.

11. Austin, *Politics in Ghana, 1946–1960* (London and New York: Oxford University Press, 1964), p. 364.

12. Corruption that has been systematized and institutionalized, according to some, need not have a debilitating effect upon the

developing economy. See Nathaniel H. Leff, "Economic Development Through Bureaucratic Corruption," *The American Behavioral Scientist,* VIII, No. 3 (November, 1964), 8–14.

13. See the summary of the *Report of the Commission of Enquiry into the Affairs of the Cocoa Purchasing Company* (the Jibowu Commission), in Austin, *op. cit.,* pp. 341–42, n 25. See also Nkrumah, *Autobiography* . . ., chap. xxii.

II. KWAME NKRUMAH: THE POLITICAL MAN

1. Examples of this type of coverage include: Erica Powell, *Kwame Nkrumah of the New Africa* (London: Thomas Nelson, 1965); John Phillips, *Kwame Nkrumah And The Future of Africa* (London: Faber & Faber, 1960; New York: Frederick A. Praeger, 1961); A. Fenner Brockway, "The Socialism of Nkrumah," in his *African Socialism* (London: The Bodley Head; Chester Springs, Pa.: Dufour Editions, 1963), pp. 62–88.

2. He was consistently evasive when confronted with his public remarks, both oral and written; he sought to dispose of his more vitriolic diplomatic utterances with a sweep of his hand, attempting to write the matter off with an allusion to "politics." Nkrumah's ghost writers have been identified as Professor Willie Abraham, Michael Dei-Anang, Erica Powell, Thomas Hodgkin, and H. M. Basner, among others. See also Conor Cruise O'Brien's review of *Neo-Colonialism: The Last Stage of Imperialism* in *The New Statesman,* November 26, 1965, pp. 831–32.

3. It is most doubtful that Nkrumah at any time gave priority to the "nation-building" task that is currently ascribed to leaders in developing areas. He was far too preoccupied with the machine-building task.

4. "One of my pleasures in London was to buy a copy of the *Daily Worker,* the only paper I really enjoyed reading . . ." (Nkrumah, *Autobiography* . . ., p. 49.) See also W. Arthur Lewis, *Politics in West Africa* (London: Allen & Unwin, 1965), p. 27; and *The Report of the Commission of Enquiry into Disturbances in the Gold Coast, 1948* (the Watson Report) (London: HMSO, 1948), pp. 17–20. The relevant passages from that Report are also cited in Nkrumah, *Autobiography* . . ., pp. 85–86. The Watson assessment of Nkrumah's Communist affinities remains one of the shrewdest appraisals ever made of a political leader before he had an opportunity to unfold his program.

5. See Nkrumah, *Autobiography* . . ., p. 45. The associates and contacts during the London years included Bankole Akpata, Ashie Nikoe, Wallace Johnson, Awooner Renner, Aka Adjei, Kojo Botsio, and T. R. Makonnen. He also had contacts with Jomo

Kenyatta, Fenner Brockway, and, very fleetingly, with M. S. M. Apithy, Léopold Senghor, Lamine Guèye, and Félix Houphouet-Boigny of French-speaking Africa.

6. John Phillips, *op. cit.*, p. 38. See also Bretton, "Current Political Thought and Practice in Ghana," p. 52.

7. *Towards Colonial Freedom* (London: Heinemann, 1962), p. ix. For the Declaration, see Appendix. It appears that the young Nkrumah was far more impressed with the radical teaching of elements in the British Communist Party than he was with the comparatively moderate teachings advanced by the Fabian Colonial Bureau which also sought to assist and to influence him.

8. *Some Essential Features of Nkrumaism* (Accra: The Spark Publications; London: Lawrence and Wishart, 1964), p. 4.

9. *Debates*, October 16, 1961, col. 54.

10. *The Times* (London), March 5, 1966. See also *The Rebirth of Ghana* (Accra: The Ministry of Information on behalf of the National Liberation Council, 1966), p. 44; Rolf Italiaander, *The New Leaders of Africa* (London: Prentice-Hall International, 1961), p. 238; and "Ju-Ju Adviser For Nkrumah," *Sunday Telegraph* (London), April 3, 1966. The name of the adviser was Alhaji Sekou, or Nyame of Kankan; see Baidoe-Ansah, *The Ghanaian Times*, March 31, 1966. Nyame was mentioned in Nkrumah's will (*The Ghanaian Times*, April 28, 1966). For evidence that a fetish priestess was also consulted by Nkrumah, see Nana Oparebeah before Apaloo Commission, *The Ghanaian Times* (Accra), June 2, 1966; *Daily Graphic* (Accra), June 2, 1966; and *Evening News* (Accra), June 1, 1966. See also accounts of Nkrumah's use of Alhaji Nourou Tali of Dakar to influence the outcome of the 1965 Conference of the Organization of African Unity, in *Ghana Today* (Accra: Ministry of External Affairs), X, No. 11, 4.

Following the overthrow, the National Liberation Council ordered inquiries to be made into Nkrumah's public affairs and his properties, and into the conduct of other officials, trade-union leaders, officers of the Workers Brigade, etc. Unless otherwise indicated, references in these notes (as above) to press statements made after the coup by Nkrumah's erstwhile associates relate to testimony before one of the several commissions of inquiry. For purposes of this book, the most important commissions were those headed by Justices Apaloo and Ollenu.

11. Chapter V of *Consciencism* (London: Heinemann, 1964) may have been produced in an attempt to update the view on man and society presented in the preceding books published under Nkrumah's name.

12. W. Arthur Lewis, who came to know Nkrumah intimately as an

economic adviser, offers some very cogent observations on this theme, though he does not apply them to any West African leader in particular (*op. cit.*, pp. 62–63). The *Ghana Evening News* fawned on Nkrumah: "He is sincere, modest and dedicated to the service of his people of Africa—wanting NOTHING for himself personally—NOTHING whatever," (April 29, 1965).

13. See Heinz Eulau, *The Behavioral Persuasion in Politics* (New York: Random House, 1963), p. 96, on the "fallacy of cultural correlation."

14. This would suggest that if terms like "one-party state" are used to describe Ghana, the term must be modified to indicate the possibility that high-level decisions and policies are not necessarily formulated with Ghana in mind.

15. See Nkrumah's reasons for using the word "spark" (i.e., Lenin's *Iskra*), in *West Africa*, November 27, 1965, p. 1333. See also the style and contents of his earlier book *Towards Colonial Freedom*.

16. Nkrumah, *Autobiography* . . ., p. 57.

17. June 11, 1965. See also letter to the Editor, signed Thomas Hodgkin, in *The Times* (London), March 5, 1966: "Whatever may happen to the term 'Nkrumahism' [sic], there is, I believe, little doubt that the complex of radical Pan Africanist ideas of which Dr. Nkrumah has during the past 20 years become the best known exponent is no more likely to wither away than the ideas of Robespierre or Jefferson, of Mazzini or Sun Yat-sen."

18. See The Reverend Stephen Dzirasa, *Political Thought of Kwame Nkrumah* (Accra: Guinea Press, n.d. [probably 1961 or 1962]), pp. 14 ff. Elspeth Huxley wrote that Nkrumah "beats the drums of race-hatred, as a device to get into power." (*Four Guineas* [London: Chatto & Windus, 1954], p. 82.) I dismiss as substantively irrelevant to the question of Nkrumah's political orientation on matters of race his willingness to employ and associate with whites.

19. *West Africa*, January 29, 1966, p. 133; for Dei-Anang's comments on that broadcast, see *Daily Graphic*, March 28, 1966. The writings of DuBois certainly influenced Nkrumah in this regard.

20. Under Nkrumah, Ghana harbored political refugees, including exiled opposition leaders from such countries as Senegal, Ivory Coast, Upper Volta, Niger, Togo, Dahomey, Cameroon, and Nigeria. In secret training camps, saboteurs were trained for action in their home countries. Groups dedicated to the overthrow of Houphouet-Boigny, Yaméogo, Diori, Balewa, and others received financial support from Nkrumah personally—the source being state funds.

21. Nkrumah, *Autobiography* . . ., Appendix B, especially point 7. See also Colin Legum, in W. H. Friedland and Carl G. Rosberg,

Jr. (eds.), *African Socialism* Stanford, Calif.: Stanford University Press, 1964), pp. 135–36.

22. Nkrumah, *Autobiography* . . ., Appendix A.
23. *Ibid.*, p. x.
24. Nkrumah, *I Speak of Freedom*, p. 113.
25. Nkrumah, *Africa Must Unite*, p. 76.
26. *Ibid.*, p. 82.
27. *Ibid.*
28. *Ibid.*, pp. 83–84.
29. Nkrumah, *I Speak of Freedom*, chap. x.

III. BUILDING THE POLITICAL MACHINE (I)

1. Essential features of the Independence Constitution may be found in "The Ghana (Constitution) Order in Council, 1957," in G. E. Metcalfe, *Great Britain and Ghana, Documents of Ghana History, 1807–1957*. (London and Legon: Thomas Nelson, for the University of Ghana, 1964), pp. 729–35.
2. For a legal analysis of the arrangements, see William B. Harvey, *Law and Social Change in Ghana* (Princeton, N.J.: Princeton University Press, 1966), pp. 141–44.
3. Nkrumah, *I Speak of Freedom*, p. 77. See also *A New Charter for the Civil Service* (White Paper No. 2; Accra, 1960).
4. Austin, *op. cit.*, is by far the best source on the history of the Nkrumah opposition; see especially chap. vi.
5. *Ibid.*, pp. 373 ff.
6. W. Arthur Lewis, *op. cit.*, p. 27. In June, 1965, in a call for "new blood" for Parliament, *The Ghanaian Times* allowed that before independence, "for strategic reasons," the ideological positions of the party were not clearly marked out. It is for this and other reasons that the possibility of Nkrumah's having originally been a Communist should not be dismissed without further investigation. See Fenner Brockway, *op. cit.*, pp. 62–63.
7. Huxley, *op. cit.*, p. 85.
8. See Bretton, "Current Political Thought and Practice."
9. See Nkrumah's Address on the Motion of Approval of the Independence Constitution, November 12, 1956, in *I Speak of Freedom*, chap. x.
10. Austin, *op. cit.*, pp. 371 ff.
11. Geoffrey Bing way well be considered the legal mastermind of the political machine. See *West Africa*, April 30, 1966, p. 481; also B. Kwaw-Swanzy, in *Daily Graphic*, May 5, 1966.
12. Austin, *op. cit.*, p. 378.
13. *Ibid.*, pp. 379–80. The Regional Assemblies Act of 1958 set up the regional bodies, and the Constitutional (Amendment) Act of

1959, clause 10, dissolved them. The same Act extended the powers of the Prime Minister over the theretofore protected Public and Judicial Services.

14. In one case, when action by the "executive" contravened existing constitutional and statutory provisions, Parliament was simply induced to pass legislation eliminating the obstructions. See Harvey, *op. cit.*, p. 298. The incident amply illustrates Nkrumah's usurpation of legality—his use of legal means to increase his own power and to diminish the power of the legislative and judicial bodies.

15. Clause 2, section 1, of the Preventive Detention Act. There appear to have been approximately 2,000 detainees between 1958 and early 1966, during which period the Act was in effect. The only documentary index to the total number of detainees which I was able to locate, prior to the coup, was in the *Annual Report on the Treatment of Offenders, 1962* (Accra: Ministry of Information and Broadcasting, 1965), p. 15, Table 42. Under "Other Offences," the report lists a total of 6,662 prisoners, the largest share from Ashanti and from countries other than Ghana. Appendix 1 (p. 31) gives a total of 1,672.53 as the daily average for the principal detention center, Nsawam Medium Security Prison, and the total of 428.22 as the daily average at Usher Fort, used for maximum security detainees. Under total "detainees," the report gives no more than 31 at Nsawam, 152 at Usher Fort, and a total of 363 detainees. That this figure was false emerges clearly from examination of the different sets of figures given for detainees on pp. 12–13, where the daily average for detainees during 1962 is given as 567; Nsawam is credited with fewer than 2 detainees per day. There was also a sharp increase in prison staff during the year 1962 (p. 5).

16. Harvey, *op. cit.*, pp. 57, 59–61.

17. In 1951, Nkrumah was reported to have said that there was no need to hold a debate on a constitution. When the time comes, he said, a constitution can be found in the back of any textbook on government.

18. Austin, *op. cit.*, pp. 387–88. The failure to distinguish between nominal, ascriptive election objectives and those actually motivating voters is one major flaw in all accounts of elections and referenda in Ghana. Also, election results, registration figures, etc., are accepted with insufficient caution and reservations. The published "results" were as follows: for the republic constitution, 1,008,740, or 88.5 per cent; against the republic constitution, 131,425, or 11.5 per cent; for Nkrumah, 1,016,076, or 89.1 per cent; for Danquah, 124,623, or 10.9 per cent. (Austin, *op. cit.*, p. 394.)

19. Article 55, section 1. For the text of the republic constitution, see David Apter, *Ghana in Transition* (New York: Atheneum, 1963), Appendix A; and Harvey, *op. cit.*, Appendix II.
20. Article 55, section 5.
21. Article 51, section 2.
22. Republic constitution, Article 45, sections 1 and 3.
23. *Debates*, August 24, 1960, cols. 899–902; August 25, 1960, cols. 903–4. In November, 1956, Nkrumah had assured Parliament that "Minority rights [will] be respected. Opposition members in the Assembly [will] be able to raise questions which seem to them in the national interest." (Nkrumah, *I Speak of Freedom*, p. 79.)
24. For a rather literal and uncritical, perhaps even somewhat misleading, account of the legal and constitutional state of affairs under Nkrumah, see L. Rubin and P. Murray, *The Constitution and Government of Ghana* (London: Sweet & Maxwell, 1961).
25. The amendment in question, 183A, addressed itself to "Any person who with intent to bring the President into hatred, ridicule, or contempt publishes any defamatory or insulting matter, whether by writing, word of mouth *or in any other manner whatsoever* concerning the President. [Italics added.]" See *Debates*, October 13, 1961, col. 22.
26. *Debates*, October 13, 1961, cols. 25–26.
27. *Ibid.*, cols. 28–31.
28. *Ibid.*, col. 31.
29. *Ibid.*, col. 32.
30. In practice, in the succeeding years, public criticism of certain limited policy matters was allowed, but never if directly against the President himself, and only through inference in relatively insensitive areas such as hoarding, mismanagement in certain industries, etc.
31. *Debates*, October 16, 1961, col. 36. On that occasion, Gbedemah attacked the Preventive Detention Act, which several years earlier he had advocated and defended. He left Ghana immediately following the attack. The relevant provisions were Article 48 of the constitution (presidential pardon), and sections 242 and 245 of the Criminal Procedure Code, amended as of 1961.
32. Criminal Procedure (Amendment) Act of 1961, Article 91.
33. On one occasion, one close collaborator of Nkrumah's, showing me a copy of a book on the CIA which he had received from Nkrumah, suggested that henceforth he would have to be careful in his contacts with Americans, for all Americans, he sighed, were potential CIA agents. To this I replied in a similar vein, "How can anyone know that you are not also an agent of the

CIA or of some other similar service?" There was no answer.

34. *Debates,* June 6, 1962, col. 568.

35. *Ibid.,* col. 551. The last Attorney General under Nkrumah, Kwaw-Swanzy, appears to have had a rather low opinion of the way in which the PDA was implemented: "There were cases . . . where people were taken by some persons, notably District Commissioners and the Security Service men, and kept in police custody where they were forgotten because there was no occasion to ask about them." (*The Ghanaian Times,* May 5, 1966.)

36. *Ibid.* What the hapless man had said was, of course, true. The "Dr." was honorary, conferred upon Nkrumah by his alma mater, Lincoln University, in 1951.

37. During the debate, the Minister of Justice suggested that in Ghana political crimes were equated with nonpolitical crimes. (*Debates,* June 13, 1962, col. 789.)

38. MP's W. A. Wiafe and P. K. Quaidoo were both detained although they were members of the supposedly ruling CPP. See also *Ghana Gazette,* September 2, 1960, p. 153, for accounts of detention of Joe Appiah and I. Asigri.

39. Section 1, subsection 1.

40. This was triggered by the famous trial of the one-time CPP leaders Tawia Adamafio, Coffie Crabbe, and Ako Adjei, plus others, on charges of conspiracy against the state and an attempt on Nkrumah's life. See Austin, *op. cit.,* pp. 413 ff. Reference is to the Criminal Procedure (Amendment) Act of 1961 as amended in subsection 2.

41. Article 1.

42. Article 1A, section 1.

43. Article 45, as amended. In March, 1964, Nkrumah removed three judges from the Supreme Court and one judge from the High Court; see "One-Party State Referendum," in *Bulletin of the International Commission of Jurists,* No. 24 (December, 1965), pp. 20–21. For the text of the amendment, and for a most interesting and revealing commentary on the alleged issues in the referendum, see the Ministry of Information and Broadcasting, *Toward the Referendum* (Accra, 1964).

44. Article 18, as amended.

45. Criminal Procedure (Amendment) Act of 1964; see *Toward the Referendum,* pp. 6–10. On the "Winneba jury," see testimony of C. D. K. Adjei, Principal Executive Officer, President's Office, before the Apaloo Commission, in *Ghana Today,* May 4, 1966, p. 8.

46. According to Kwaw-Swanzy, Nkrumah's last Attorney General, although the Attorney General's Office was required under the PDA to furnish detainees with the reasons for their detention,

this was done only once, when Geoffrey Bing was Attorney General. "After that," said Kwaw-Swanzy, "nobody ever asked the Attorney General's Office to have anything to do with the Act." (*The Ghanaian Times*, May 5, 1966.)

47. Ghana, *The Annual Estimates for 1965* (Part I: The Consolidated Fund), Vol. XIII: *Interior*, pp. 3, 25; and Vol. I.: *The President*, p. 3.

IV. BUILDING THE POLITICAL MACHINE (II)

1. Ayeh-Kumi, *Rebirth of Ghana*, p. 45. Nkrumah collected his annual salary at the beginning of each year. (Major General Kotoka, *The Ghanaian Times*, March 25, 1966.) See also Krobo Edusei before the Apaloo Commission, in *The Times* (London), March 30, 1966, p. 9. Estimates of Nkrumah's total accumulated wealth, including bank accounts, properties at home and abroad, held alone and jointly with others, and under other names, ranged as high as £40 million. (Apaloo Commission, *The Ghanaian Times*, April 22, 1966.) One method of personal enrichment involved unauthorized lending of sums from government funds and their eventual repayment into Nkrumah's private accounts. (T. K. Impraim, *Daily Graphic*, May 6, 1966.)

2. Ayeh-Kumi, *The Ghanaian Times*, March 22 and 23, 1966; also Amoaka-Atta, *Evening News*, March 24, 1966. The former Minister of Finance revealed that among other large contracts handled by him at his sole discretion, Nkrumah had also unilaterally awarded the contract for "Job 600," the £8 million structure built especially for the 1965 Organization of African Unity summit conference, the £7.5-million shipbuilding and dockyard project at Tema, and the £15-million airport at Tamale. It is unlikely that the complex financial dealings of Nkrumah can ever be completely uncovered and sorted out. For evidence that the funds collected were diverted from the party to Nkrumah, see Ayeh-Kumi, *Daily Graphic*, March 22, 1966. See also *The Ghanaian Times*, April 22, 1966; and Harry Dodoo, *Daily Graphic*, April 29, 1966.

3. Bourret, *op. cit.*, p. 180.

4. Ghana, *The Annual Estimates for 1963–64* (Part I), Vol. XVI, Appendix VI. Nkrumah interpreted development needs rather liberally, including under that rubric: security walls surrounding his residences, his private menagerie, various personal as well as official obligations, and certain foreign-affairs projects, mainly covert operations elsewhere in Africa. See testimony before the Apaloo Commission, *inter alia*; also "Financial State-

ment, 1965," p. 6, in *The Budget, 1965.* See also *Annual Estimates for 1965* (Part I), Vol. I, p. 19.

5. See *Commission of Enquiry into Mr. Braimah's Resignation and Allegations Arising Therefrom* (The Korsah Commission) (Accra, 1954).

6. Bourret, *op. cit.,* p. 180.

7. *Ibid.*

8. Quoted in *The Ghanaian Times,* March 25, 1966.

9. *The Ghanaian Times,* May 7, 1966; and *Daily Graphic,* May 6, 1966. See also Ayeh-Kumi, *The Ghanaian Times,* March 25, 1966; Impraim, *Daily Graphic,* April 16, 1966, and May 6, 1966; and *The Ghanaian Times,* April 16, 1966.

10. Police Commissioner Harlley, in *The Ghanaian Times,* March 11, 1966.

11. The Chieftaincy (Recognition) Act of 1957 prepared the ground, worked over with the aid of subsequent regulatory legislation. The deterioration of the economic position of the chiefs is traced in Harvey, *op. cit.,* chap ii. See also Impraim on Nkrumah's subsidy of the Asantehene's medical expenses—*The Ghanaian Times,* May 6, 1966.

12. Samuel P. Huntington, "Political Development and Political Decay," *World Politics,* XVII, No. 3 (April, 1965), 416.

13. Evidence before the Effah, Apaloo, and Ezu-Crabbe commissions brought to light the pattern of bribery; key leaders appear to have been Margaret Martei, Hawa Banda, Susanna Al-Hassan, Grace Ayensu, Suzanne Halm, Victoria Nyarku, Sophia Doku, Lily Appiah, Christiana Wilmot. See *Evening News,* May 5, 1966, on the £2,000 gift to Hawa Banda. By all appearances, trading women in Ghana seem to have behaved politically very much like their sisters in Nigeria; see Bretton, in Spiro (ed.), *op. cit.,* especially p. 61.

14. David Apter writes, in W. J. Hanna, *Independent Black Africa* (Chicago: Rand McNally, 1964), pp. 264–65: "The major achievement of the CPP in Ghana was the organization and maintenance of an effective mass political organization." Seeking to justify the 1951 transfer of power from Britain to Nkrumah, the then Governor Arden-Clarke wrote in 1958: "Nkrumah and his party had the mass of the people behind them and there was no other party with appreciable public support to which one could turn." Quoted in Bourret, *op. cit.,* p. 175.) See also Harvey, *op. cit.,* pp. 322–23, 342. Even as detached an observer as E. N. Omaboe succumbed to the myth. Reviewing accomplishments in Ghana between 1951 and 1957, he wrote: "With government also passing into the hands of a party charged with exceptional dynamism the lead [over other African states]

was translated into concrete achievements in the spheres of economic and social development." (W. B. Birmingham, I. Neustadt, and E. N. Omaboe [eds.], *The Economy of Ghana* [London: Allen & Unwin, 1966], p. 21.)

15. Apter, who is quoted above as supporting the mass-organization thesis, recognized with regard to the 1951 election that "the attitude of the local chiefs was of great importance." (*Ghana in Transition*, p. 199.) It appears that traditional organization, rather than party organization, was the key element in the climb to power by Nkrumah and his supporters. It would be a mistake, however, to draw far-reaching conclusions concerning the political power potential of the chiefs.

16. See statement to the press by John Tettegah, March 10, 1966. See also B. A. Bentum, *The Ghanaian Times*, March 2, 1966. A description of the formal structure of the TUC may be found in Kwaw Ampah, "Focus on Ghana T.U.C.," *The Spark*, January 21, 1966. Total membership in 1965 was claimed to be approximately 400,000. Technically, the TUC was an arm of the CPP; politically, it was not.

17. C. C. Baah, *Debates*, February 23, 1961, col. 197.

18. *The Ghanaian Times*, February 27, 1961. After the coup, when asked about his membership in the CPP, Tettegah replied: "I could tell you from my own assessment that banned party never existed over some years now since Nkrumah took direct personal power, so it doesn't matter if you are a member of this party or not." (Press statement, March 10, 1966.)

19. Major General H. T. Alexander, *African Tightrope: My Two Years as Nkrumah's Chief of Staff* (London: Pall Mall Press, 1965; New York: Frederick A. Praeger, 1966), pp. 91, 147–48.

20. See Kwaku Boateng, *The Ghanaian Times*, March 24, 1966; Amoako-Atta, *ibid.*, March 25, 1966; Edusei, *The Times* (London), March 30, 1966, p. 9; Mohamed Fouad Fattal, *Daily Graphic*, March 18, 1966; Kweku Akwei, *The Ghanaian Times*, March 26, 1966; F. E. Tachie-Menson, *ibid.*, April 1, 1966.

21. Boateng, *The Ghanaian Times*, March 24, 1966.

22. Ayeh-Kumi, *Rebirth of Ghana*, pp. 42–44.

23. The only politically potent group was the one organized by Tawia Adamafio, largely on his own. After Adamafio's fall, Nkrumah took special care not to allow another such group to form. (See Austin, *op. cit.*, p. 407, n 77.) The Adamafio group, it should be noted, was a singularly cynical, nonideological assemblage of political climbers, stray civil servants who could not afford to turn down Adamafio's invitation, and genuine conspirators. A major center for production of philosophic formulations was the Department of Philosophy at Legon.

24. Colin Legum, in Friedland and Rosberg (eds.), *op. cit.*, p. 140.
25. Austin, *op. cit.*, pp. 405 ff.; Apter *Ghana In Transition*, pp. 348 ff.
26. See especially, *Dawn Broadcast*, April 8, 1961 (Accra: Ghana Information Services, 1961); excerpts are given in Austin, *op. cit.*, pp. 403–4.
27. Nkrumah ordering reassignment of responsibilities within the party reminds one of Hitler, who, in his last days, ordered non-existing armies to attack illusory targets. See Apter, in James S. Coleman and Carl G. Rosberg, Jr. (eds.), *Political Parties and National Integration in Tropical Africa* (Berkeley, Calif.: University of California Press, 1964), p. 297.
28. See chap. v, "Set Theoretic Terms."
29. Colin Legum notes that in 1961, soon after Nkrumah had lifted some of the radicals to prominence, he discovered their administrative incompetence. (In Friedland and Rosberg (eds.), *op. cit.*, p. 150. Kodwo Addison, Director of the Ideological Institute at Winneba, was an example.
30. Vernon Van Dyke, *Political Science: A Philosophical Analysis* (Stanford, Calif.: Stanford University Press, 1960), p. 173.
31. For a critical assessment of *Conscientism*, see Manfred Halpern, "African Socialism: Some Unanswered Questions," *Africa Report*, November, 1965, pp. 60–62. See also Colin Legum, in Friedland and Rosberg (eds.), *op. cit.*; Charles F. Andrain, "Patterns of African Socialist Thought," *African Forum*, I, No. 3 (Winter, 1966), 48–49.
32. Apter, in Coleman and Rosberg (eds.), *op. cit.*, p. 308.
33. According to the former Minister of Housing, Nkrumah built two palaces "for the chiefs of Nkroful and Nsuayem" with public funds. Nkrumah was the chief of Nsuayem and the Tufuhene of Nkroful in the Nzima tradition. (Tachie-Menson, *Daily Graphic*, April 1, 1966; see also Italiaander, *op. cit.*, p. 227.)
34. The principal engineer of the cult and probable originator of the Messiah myth appears to have been Tawia Adamafio (when serving as Minister for Presidential Affairs); for his admission of this before the Apaloo Commission, see *Daily Graphic*, June 2, 1966; and *Evening News*, June 1, 1966. See especially Tawia Adamafio, *A Portrait of Osagyefo . . .* (Broadcast, September 21, 1960) (Accra: Government Printer, 1960).
35. Italiaander, *op. cit.*, p. 228. The only prominent Nkrumaist who publicly (in *The Ghanaian Times*) sought to discourage the "adulation" of Nkrumah was Professor W. E. Abraham. For that, he was strongly attacked by Eric Heymann in the *Evening News*. (See Dennis Duerden, letter to the Editor, *The Observer* [London], May 1, 1966.)

36. *The Ghanaian Times*, November 27, 1964.
37. *Ibid.*, December 7, 1964.
38. In 1965, a State Publishing Corporation was created to supervise and control all publishing and distribution of all materials in Ghana and abroad. Michael Dei-Anang was Chairman, Professor Abraham a Board member. (*Handbook on State Corporations* [Accra: State Enterprises Secretariat, 1965], pp. 40–41. See also David H. Bayley, *Public Liberties in the New States* [Chicago: Rand McNally, 1964], p. 56.)
39. Anon., "Law in the Building of Socialism" (I), *The Spark*, January 22, 1965, p. 2.
40. Address by Nkrumah on the occasion of the opening of the Institute of African Studies at Legon, October 26, 1963.
41. See anon., *op. cit., The Spark*; and Robert B. Seidman, "Law in the Building of Socialism" (II and III), *The Spark*, February 5 and February 12, 1965. The first article was also said to have been authored by Seidman, who was subsequently appointed Presidential Professor of Law at Legon. Publication of all three pieces was a result of Nkrumah's personal initiative; he insisted on publication of these views as a condition for employment at the University of Ghana. (See also Pritt, *The Spark*, January 29, 1965, and February 12, 1965.) For another example of a Nkrumaist rationalization about law and legality, see "Socialist Progress and the Judiciary," *The Spark*, May 21, 1965.
42. *Towards the Referendum*, pp. 9–10.
43. Harvey, *op. cit.*, pp. 172–73.
44. Author's interview with Nkrumah, January 15, 1965.
45. Pritt, *op. cit.*
46. Nkrumah, "The Role of Our Universities," Speech delivered at the University of Ghana, February 24, 1963 (Accra: Ministry of Information and Broadcasting, 1963), pp. 1–3. The University of Ghana Act of 1961, section 3, stated that "The principal officers of the University shall be the Chancellor, the Chairman of the University Council and the Vice-Chancellor." Section 4: "The President shall hold the office of Chancellor and as such shall be the Head of the University."
47. The aversion to scientific—i.e., objective—social, political, and economic research on the part of regimes claiming to be scientifically oriented is noteworthy. As far as research was concerned, Nkrumah's commitment to scientific research extended to giving support to the Atomic Energy Project and to applied industrial and agricultural research. While the Atomic Energy Project was allocated £G500,000 in development funds for 1965, the Humanities Section on Social and Economic Research of the Ghana Academy of Science was closed down. No government funds were allo-

cated to purely theoretical research to advance ideology, education, or social philosophy. The closest approximation to such research was to be found in the research sections of the departments of Economics and Philosophy at the University of Ghana which produced *Neo-Colonialism: The Last Stage of Imperialism* and parts of *Consciencism*). The Institute of African Studies under a most loyal Nkrumaist Director, Thomas Hodgkin, carefully refrained from using funds for scientific analysis of the benefactor's regime. The £G250,000 allocated in 1965 to the Kwame Nkrumah Institute at Winneba were of course in politically safe hands. All in all, the most worth-while social-science research project, in terms of long-range benefits to the development of Ghana, was the Ford Foundation–financed—though nominally sponsored by the Ghana Academy of Sciences—Study of Contemporary Ghana, the first volume of which appeared in 1965: Birmingham, Neustadt and Omaboe (eds.), *The Economy of Ghana*. Although of considerable value to an understanding of the basic structure and problems of the economy of Ghana and devastating in its implied criticism of Nkrumaist economic policy, the study avoids a frontal attack. The Nkrumah issue is ignored; at best it is treated obliquely in vague references to "politicians" who fail to take civil servants' advice (pp. 460–61).

48. *Bulletin of the International Commission of Jurists,* No. 24 (December, 1965), pp. 21–23. See also "Can Students Expose Teachers?," *The Ghanaian Times,* November 25, 1964; and "University and Academic Freedom," *ibid.,* January 27, 1965. The Scholarship Secretariat, also under the President, was to review all scholarships on the basis of "satisfactory performance and good conduct." Although this was not applied as diligently as had been intended, the knowledge that the power had been granted had a inhibiting effect on the students. The relationship between the University and the President is eloquently illustrated by the following excerpt from an open letter to "Osagyefo," published in *The Ghanaian Times,* November 24, 1965, by a professor who had been arrested in 1964, on Nkrumah's orders, detained for one year, released, and then permitted to resume a position at the University: "I take this opportunity to thank you for having enough confidence in me to restore me back to the University of Ghana. I am fully aware that as a result of my rash approach on a few issues before my departure for India in June, 1956, it has since been very easy for my ill-wishers to cloud me with a series of unfounded allegations." Prior to his arrest, the professor had been an enthusiastic supporter of the President on campus.

49. The Civil Service (Amendment) Act of 1965 abolished the Civil

Service Commission, transferring its functions to the presidential Establishment Secretariat. The work of the new Secretariat was to be carried out "under the direct responsibility of the President." (See *Debates*, September 6, 1965, cols. 463–64.) Nkrumah himself commented on the situation prior to 1960: "Disagreeable to us in the extreme [the entrenched clauses in the independence constitution] had the effect of surrounding each civil servant with a barricade which the government was allowed to scale only with the greatest difficulty." Nkrumah, *Africa Must Unite*, pp. 84–85, 87–96.) In the course of my first interview with Nkrumah, in August, 1956, he made a point of relating to me how a particular order from him, to purchase a road-grading machine, had been sidetracked by a Permanent Secretary for more than six months under a variety of what Nkrumah regarded as subterfuges.

v. THE FINAL YEAR

1. Deutsch, *The Nerves of Government: Models of Political Communication and Control* (New York: The Free Press of Glencoe, 1963), pp. 178 ff.
2. Adamafio appears to have operated on the assumption that Nkrumah's attention could be dulled by applications of massive doses of flattery. While attempting to build his own machine in the party, administration, and elsewhere, he excelled in sycophantic hyperbole. See Adamafio, *A Portrait of Osagyefo* . . . .
3. See *The Ghanaian Times*, March 13, 1965.
4. *Annual Estimates for 1965* (Part I), Vol. I, p. 7. See also E. N. Omaboe, *The Ghanaian Times*, March 4, 1966; and Michael Dei-Anang, press conference, *Daily Graphic*, March 28, 1966. The Contingency Fund was meant to cover expenditures incurred before the National Assembly could make necessary authorization. In practice, Nkrumah used the £2 million as a slush fund on "all sorts of things" without legislative authorization or accounting. (T. K. Impraim, *The Ghanaian Times*, April 16, 1966; see also *ibid.*, May 6, 1966.)
5. Michael Dei-Anang, *Daily Graphic*, March 28, 1966. The 1965 *Financial Statement*, p. 6, shows, under additional "Development" provisions for the President: £67,700 for security wall at Flagstaff House; £96,400 for menagerie . . . and aquarium at Flagstaff House; £70,000 for minor construction at Flagstaff House and at State House; and £88,000 for National Gliding School (under the direction of Hanna Reitsch). See also C. D. K. Adjei, *The Ghanaian Times*, April 15, 1966.
6. The Regional Commissioners, key elements in the personal ma-

chine, also were assigned internal-security responsibilities; see *Annual Estimates for 1965* (Part I), p. 109. See also Baidoo-Ansah, *Daily Graphic*, March 30, 1966.

7. What had been known as the Presidential Guard Regiment had secretly been expanded, trained, and equipped with weapons whose firepower was superior to those at the disposal of the regular forces. The plan seems to have called for elevation of that unit to the level of a strategic security force following the Hitlerian or Stalinist models. See *Sunday Telegraph* (London), April 17, 1966; Lieutenant General Ankrah, *The Ghanaian Times*, March 8, 1966. In all, Nkrumah's security force consisted of the following units: Presidential Guard (Special Force), Security Service, Criminal Investigation Department, personal informers, regular police, the regular armed forces, the Workers Brigade, and armed party activists. There also was the private bodyguard.

At first, it was announced that the Ministry had been renamed the Ministry of Civil Defense. Under the new arrangement, Kofi Baako was handed the task of administering the Workers Brigade; he also was to train that unwieldy body to assume the function of an auxiliary civilian defense force akin to similar organizations found in Eastern Europe. For that purpose, £G350,000 were allocated to "Defense" in 1965; see, *Financial Statement, 1965*, p. 7.

8. Kofi Baako, news conference, March 22, 1966; reported in *The Times* (London), March 23, 1966.

9. Ayeh-Kumi, in *Rebirth of Ghana*, pp. 43–45. A great deal of evidence emerged after the coup indicating that Nkrumah used the Bank of Ghana and other financial institutions as instruments of political pressure. See also testimony before Effah (Housing) Commission, *inter alia*; Impraim, *The Ghanaian Times*, April 16, 1966.

10. *Economic Survey, 1963* (Accra: Ministry of Information and Broadcasting, 1964), pp. 116–17, Tables 82 and 84; *Economic Survey, 1964*, pp. 105–6, Tables 73, 74, 75.

11. *O and M* [Organization and Methods] *Bulletin*, No. 4 (October, 1962), p. 5.

12. See Alexander, *op. cit.*, chap. ix (e.g., p. 103): "The officers and Ministry of Defence had to be pretty versatile in juggling their financial figures and organisational charts because new units were apt to be dreamed up overnight."

13. Deutsch, *op. cit.*, pp. 54–55.

14. Overreliance on tables of precedence, manuals, and rank order has long been the bane of political analysts. If such materials

are mentioned or shown here, it is only to illustrate the formal structure.

15. *Ghana Gazette*, August 5, 1960, p. 71.
16. *The Ghanaian Times*, December 9, 1964.
17. Alexander, *op. cit.*, The Ambassador at that time was G. M. Rodionov. One of Nkrumah's earliest benefactors and financial advisers was the Greek businessman and multimillionaire A. G. Leventis, whose name does not appear in Nkrumah's publications. The history of Nkrumaist Ghana cannot be complete without a careful analysis of this man's role.
18. *Ibid.*, pp. 50 ff. and Appendix A.
19. See Dei-Anang, press conference, March 26, 1966, reported in *Daily Graphic*, March 28, 1966: "Mr. Dei-Anang said in view of the light that has been shown on the character and life of Nkrumah he would review chapter eight of his book." See also Quaison-Sackey's defense of the Nkrumaist press in his letter to me, *The Ghanaian Times*, September 13, 1965. The tone of the letter, written as he was about to assume his new role as Nkrumah's Foreign Minister, indicates that it was written and published in order to ingratiate himself with Nkrumah.
20. See Edusei, press conference, March 29, 1966, reported in *The Times* (London), March 30, 1966, p. 9. After 1961, Nkrumah permitted, probably encouraged—he could have interdicted it—a running public feud between Edusei and Kwaku Boateng; see, for example, *Debates,* June 6, 1962, cols. 585–86.
21. Quaison-Sackey: "Not much policy was made at Cabinet meetings because Nkrumah ran everything." (*The Ghanaian Times*, March 3, 1966; see also Alexander, *op. cit.*, p. 60.)
22. Office of the Planning Commission, *Seven-Year Development Plan. Annual Plan for the Second Plan Year, 1965* (Accra: Ministry for Information and Broadcasting, 1965), 2d unnumbered page. Nkrumah was Chairman, Kojo Botsio, Vice-Chairman; other members were K. Amoako-Atta, W. M. Q. Halm, E. Ayeh-Kumi, J. V. L. Phillips, J. H. Mensah, E. N. Omaboe, and A. Adomako. In some ways, this group served as one of several "inner cabinets." A good description of the formal planning process is provided by Omaboe in his contribution to Birmingham, Neustadt, and Omaboe (eds.), *op. cit.*, chap. xviii.
23. *Seven-Year Development Plan, 1963/64 to 1969/70* (Accra: Office of the Planning Commission, 1964). After the coup, Lieutenant General Ankrah commented: "For the past two years [the Seven-Year Development Plan] has existed in name [only]." (*Rebirth of Ghana*, p. 37.)
24. Reginald Green, "Four African Development Plans: Ghana,

Kenya, Nigeria, and Tanzania," *The Journal of Modern African Studies*, III, No. 2 (1965), 249–79.

25. *Ghana Yearbook, 1965* (Accra: Daily Graphic, 1965), p. 30. *Annual Estimates for 1965*, p. 26.

26. Omaboe, who played a key role in the planning process, summarizes the reasons why planning under Nkrumah did not live up to expectations: (1) The basic principles underlying the Seven-Year Plan were to be grafted onto the Ghanaian economy following Nkrumah's exposure to lectures on the successes of the Soviet Seven-Year Plan during his tour of the Soviet Union, China, and Eastern Europe in 1961. (*The Economy of Ghana, op. cit.*, pp. 450–51.) (2) For political reasons, the "government" could not persuade itself to favor one alternative over another—i.e., when a decision had to be made to opt for one project over another, "government" would opt for both. (3) "Politicians" conceived costly projects and committed the nation to their support regardless of provisions of the Plan and without careful, expert assessment of the implications for the economy. Civil servants invariably were brought in when it was too late. (4) There was a lack of clear distinctions between the functions of the cabinet and the responsibility of the planning agencies. (*Ibid.*, pp. 460–61.) (For added realism, or accuracy, one should read "Nkrumah" for "politicians," and "President's Office" for "cabinet.") Omaboe also reveals the attraction of the efficiency-minded civil servant to the streamlined dictatorial regime: "[Ghana] is fortunate in her form of government which makes it easy to take decisions which, although they may be in the national interest, nevertheless may offend certain sectional interests." (*Ibid.*, p. 22.) See also Alexander, *op. cit.*, p. 103. Dei-Anang: "It was difficult to get Nkrumah to realise that it was difficult to go on with some of his plans, unrealistic as they were." (*Daily Graphic*, March 28, 1966.)

27. Some of the worst advice in these respects came from Drevici and Sagall, with whom Nkrumah had chosen to work on major economic projects.

28. *Seven-Year Development Plan. Annual Plan for . . . 1965*, p. 23. See also *Annual Estimates for 1965* (Part I, Vol. XI: *Industries*, p. 3.

29. Contracts worth millions of pounds and profoundly affecting the economy were signed by Nkrumah, or on his orders, without the usual economic feasibility studies—e.g., the £7.6 million cocoa storage facility contract signed with Drevici. (Harry Dodoo, *Daily Graphic*, April 29, 1966.) To further these designs, the Budget Committee of the Finance Ministry was separated from the Planning Commission by a veil of secrecy.

30. *West Africa*, April 24, 1965. See also the editorials on decision-making in *The Ghanaian Times*, December 9, 1964, and May 1, 1965; and *Economic Survey*, 1964, p. 64.
31. *Debates*, February 1, 1966, col. 8.
32. Alfred Diamant, "Bureaucracy in Developmental Movement Regimes: A Bureaucratic Model for Developing Societies" (unpublished paper), p. 68. Nkrumah's strident assertions rendered analysis difficult. For example: "The party organs make the decisions, and the "government" carries them out; the government is the agent of the party. Nowhere is party supremacy more vigorously asserted than in Ghana, where Nkrumah has said of the CPP: 'It is the uniting force that guides and pilots the nation and is the nerve center of the positive struggles for African irredentism [sic]. Its supremacy cannot be challenged. The CPP is Ghana and Ghana is the CPP.'" (Rupert Emerson, in Karl W. Deutsch and William J. Foltz (eds.), *Nation-Building* [New York: Atherton Press, 1963], p. 108.) The hazards flowing from overreliance on nominal accounts concerning structure and operation of political parties in Africa, especially in Ghana, are amply illustrated in Thomas Hodgkin, *African Political Parties* (Harmondsworth: Penguin Books, 1961); see, for example, p. 99: "Within the CPP it is, I think, recognized that the responsibility for decisions rests with the Central Committee, not merely with the Life Chairman."
33. Nkrumah, *Autobiography* . . ., pp. 149 ff.
34. Sam Ikoku, address, April 23, 1965, "The Public Servant in a Socialist Administration" (Green Hill: Institute of Public Administration, 1965; mimeographed).
35. Victor Mamphey, in *The Pan-Africanist Review*, I, No. 3 (September, 1964), 96–97.
36. W. Arthur Lewis wrote: "Ghana's party pays lip service to [the objective of keeping in close touch with the rank and file] but does not really try." He suggests that it is the job of the CPP "to keep the populace in line, rather than to stimulate discussion and transmit opinion upwards." (Lewis, *op. cit.*, p. 23.) It would appear that Professor Lewis was quite close to the mark.
37. *CPP Constitution*, revised, 1965, Article 9.
38. *Ibid.*, Part IV.
39. *Ibid.*, Article 50 (b) "The supreme co-ordinating agency [of the National Party Secretariat] shall be the life Chairman/General Secretary." See also Boateng, *The Ghanaian Times*, March 24, 1966, describing the Central Committee as a "one-man show." I. A. Amihere noted that Nkrumah acted for the Central Committee (*The Ghanaian Times*, April 27, 1966.)
40. *CPP Constitution*, revised, 1965, Article 57. See also *West Africa*,

January 1, 1966, p. 19; and "Party Constitution," *Evening News*,
June 4, 1965.

41. *Debates*, February 10, 1965, cols. 955, 957.

42. See, for example, the debate on the "pass-book scandal," *Debates*,
March 24, 1965, cols. 1482, 1499–1500, 1502. The Minister of
Trade, A. Y. K. Djin, was accused of malpractice. He was first
transferred to the Ministry for Animal Husbandry (an appropriate post for a scapegoat), only to be dropped from the government shortly thereafter. (*The Ghanaian Times*, April 15, 1965.)
A few months later, Nkrumah ordered another investigation into
trade practices and appointed Professor Abraham to head the
commission. However, before he allowed the commission report
to be published, he ordered a committee of ministers and Professor Abraham to delete all references to ministers and to all
other matter that could prove embarrassing to his rule. (Kwaku
Akwei, *Evening News*, March 25, 1966; see also *Report of the
Commission of Enquiry into Trade Malpractices in Ghana*
[Abraham Commission] [Accra: Office of the President, 1966].)

43. An illustration of the problem confronting MP's was the bill
placed before the Assembly proposing a 7½ per cent increase
of the workers' contribution to the Social Security Fund. Those
who wished to object to what they knew was to the workers an
unacceptable increase could not get around the difficulty of
separating the sacred person and office of the President from the
decision quite obviously made by him. (*Debates*, February 16,
1965, cols. 107 ff.) Now and then, a skillful MP succeeded in
belling the cat; this feat was accomplished by coating the criticism of Nkrumah with flattery. Thus, one MP rose and con-
gratulated Osagyefo on his wisdom in creating the Workers Brigade, then proceeded to suggest that a Board of Governors should
be created to manage the Brigade because, he believed, "it would
be only such a body that could rid the Brigade of inefficiency,
laziness, and malingering." (*The Ghanaian Times*, September
9, 1965.)

44. *First Report From The Public Accounts Committee Of The National Assembly*, May 22, 1964; and *Second Report . . .* October
2, 1964.

45. "The Socialist Parliament," *The Spark*, May 28, 1965.

46. *Report of the Delimitation Commission* (Accra: Office of the
President, 1965), especially pp. 1–3.

47. During the first (long) Parliament, twenty-three of the boards
of forty-seven state enterprises were chaired by MP's. (*Ghana
Gazette*, March 5, 1965, p. 140; and *Handbook On State Corporations.*

48. Nkrumah, message to the National Assembly, in *The Ghanaian*

Times, May 26, 1965. To give effect to this warning, a Party-Parliamentary Disciplinary Control Committee was formed. See also the National Assembly Act of 1961 and the National Assembly (Amendment) Act of 1964.

49. Presidential Elections Act of 1965, Constitution (Amendment) Act of 1965, and Electoral Provisions Act of 1965.

50. B. F. Kusi, who had been a member of the opposition and whose repeated applications for membership in the CPP had been rejected on grounds of "disloyalty." (*Debates*, May 18, 1965, col. 12.) Kusi was one of the "irrepressibles" who would not stop giving voice to his thoughts.

51. See *Bulletin of the International Commission of Jurists*, No. 24 (December, 1965), p. 27. A story and an editorial in the *Ghanaian Times* of May 31, 1965, announced that an election originally scheduled for June 9 was to be held on June 8, 1965; see also *Evening News*, May 28, 1965. When the election was canceled abruptly—posters announcing it and identifying polling places had already been displayed in public—and a BBC commentator attempted to rationalize this about-face, the tune was changed and the unballotted, nonelected Parliament was represented in the press as Nkrumah's latest contribution to democracy. (*The Ghanaian Times*, June 5, 1965.)

52. The new, wholly captive Assembly contained 198 seats as against 104 in the old one. In one of his rare, unguarded moments, the Leader of the House, Kofi Baako, let slip that the candidates—nominally the choices of the Central Committee—should say "thank you" to Osagyefo for nominating them to stand for Parliament as party candidates. (*The Ghanaian Times*, May 31, 1965.) Investigations after the coup into the properties and financial transactions of members of the machine revealed that Nkrumah had not only become the principal employer of most of the new, hand-picked MP's, but had also bestowed extra bonuses for good (political) conduct. It was small wonder that the recipients of loans, free trips on Ghana Airways to London, graft, protection from the Special Branch, CID, etc., would loudly cheer their benefactor when he joined them in Parliament on special occasions.

53. *Debates*, August 24, 1965, col. 16. On August 26, 1965, Kofi Baako "ruled" on a point of order made by an MP, but the new partisan Speaker (Kofi Ofori Atta) failed to reprimand him. Thus the Standing Orders of the House had ceased to have effect altogether, notwithstanding the valiant efforts by the able Clerk of the House, K. B. Ayensu, to keep the institution alive. (See Ayensu, "The Deliberative Function of the National Assembly," *The Ghanaian Times*, January 28, 1965.) For a rather

unrealistic assessment of the Nkrumaist Parliament, see Jon Kraus, "Ghana's New Corporate Parliament," *Africa Report*, August, 1965, pp. 6–11. Speaking of the nonelected Parliament, Kraus found only one "political appointee" among the hand-picked new MP's (p. 11).

54. *The Ghanaian Times*, September 13, 1965.
55. *Debates*, September 6, 1965, cols. 462–63.
56. At one point during the debate, while he was being reprimanded by a spokesman of the government, Iddrissu told the Speaker: "I know my one foot is in Parliament and the other at Nsawam [the principal detention camp]. But I know no fear. I will speak; we are in Parliament." (*Ibid.*, col. 463.)
57. *The Ghanaian Times*, April 5, 1965, p. 7.
58. *Ibid.*, April 2, 1965, p. 7. The Act referred to was the Criminal Code as amended in 1961.
59. *Ibid.*
60. *Ibid.*, December 9, 1965. The occasion was the conferral of an honorary Doctor of Science degree upon Mrs. Hodgkin. The physical sciences were going to be favored over the social sciences; to that end, a Ministry of Science and Education had been set up. (See Nkrumah, *Debates*, February 1, 1966, col. 12.)
61. Nkrumah to Dapo Fatogun (Editor of the *Nigerian Sunday Express*), in *The Ghanaian Times*, June 5, 1965, p. 6.
62. *The Ghanaian Times*, October 1, 1965. In January, 1966, two additional papers were introduced, the *Daily Gazette* and the *Sunday Punch*. According to I. A. Amihere, Managing Director of the Guinea Press, the board of directors of the Guinea Press were mere puppets—Nkrumah directed press policy. (*The Ghanaian Times*, April 27, 1966.)
63. See Nkrumah, *Neo-Colonialism: The Last Stage of Imperialism.*
64. The most undisguised sycophants in the field of journalism were probably The Reverend Arthur Howarth, the "Black Dean," and Eric Heymann, Editor of the *Evening News*. Significantly, all the principal editors (T. O. Baffoe, Eric Heymann, Kofi Badu) were given free houses by Nkrumah. (Impraim, *Daily Graphic*, April 16, 1966.)
65. See Lucien W. Pye (ed.), *Communications and Political Development* (Princeton, N.J.: Princeton University Press, 1963); and Wilbur Schramm, *Mass Media and National Development: The Role of Information in the Developing Countries* (Stanford, Calif.: Stanford University Press, 1964). One basic deficiency in literature of this type is the assumption that the public reads what is written and understands it as intended. This assumption is tenuous, at best, in literate societies, and wholly misleading with regard to tropical Africa.

66. *The Spark,* March 5, 1965.
67. *Consciencism,* p. 107. "Positive action," a euphemism for strikes and civil disobedience, became Nkrumah's slogan during the early stages of his career, especially during the 1950 campaign for self-government. In 1965, it meant everything and nothing, an empty slogan.
68. *Ibid.,* pp. 111–12; on the question of authorship, see B. G. D. Folson, *The Ghanaian Times,* March 21, 1966; Professor Abraham at Apaloo Commission, *Ghana Today,* x, No. 10 (July 13, 1966), 5.
69. *Debates,* August 24, 1965, col. 43.
70. Actually, no serious attempts were undertaken during Nkrumah's rule to resolve the basic conflicts and contradictions between Marxist, Socialist, and Nkrumaist ideological prescriptions. The differences were simply swept aside with crude generalizations, slogans, and platitudes. In December, 1965, Nkrumah declared: "There is only one socialism—scientific socialism." *The Spark* added to that: "Scientific socialism as enriched and advanced in Nkrumaism." (December 24, 1965.) It appears that the term "science" was used to cover up the deficiencies in Nkrumah's ideological makeup—more generally, to cover up the chaotic nature of Nkrumaism.
71. *The Ghanaian Times,* March 13, 1965.
72. *Estimates of Charged Expenditures for 1965 . . . Consolidated Fund,* p. 12.
73. See also *Annual Estimates for 1963/64,* Vol. I, p. 115; *Annual Estimates for 1965,* Vol. I, pp. 109 ff.
74. Following reorganization in 1965, Local Government was detached from the Ministry of Justice, where it had been administered for some time and was again set up as a separate Ministry. The Local and Municipal Councils Secretariat, established in October, 1964, to give the President tighter control over a critical area of neglect, corruption, and confusion, was returned to the Ministry of Local Government. Politically, this had become feasible with the redrawing of district and constituency lines and a tightening of the regional and party organizations—i.e., of the personal political machine. The over-all supervision was still in the President's hands, the critical lines of communication and control ending in his office.

VI. EVALUATION: THE EFFECTS OF PERSONAL RULE ON GOVERNMENT AND ADMINISTRATION

1. For a useful discussion of problems related to the development of politics, see Herbert J. Spiro, *The Primacy of Politics in Africa*

(New York: Random House, 1966), pp. 150-169; see also Samuel P. Huntington, *op. cit.*

2. Deutsch, *op. cit.*, pp. 182 ff. See also Wiener, *The Human Use of Human Beings.*

3. Arthur M. Schlesinger, Jr., *A Thousand Days* (Boston: Houghton Mifflin, 1965), p. 613.

4. David Easton, *A Framework For Political Analysis* (Englewood Cliffs, N.J.: Prentice-Hall, 1965), p. 94.

5. Huntington, *op. cit.*

6. Lewis, *op. cit.*, p. 60.

7. *Ibid.*

8. The formula used in Bretton, *Power and Stability in Nigeria*, p. 3.

9. Ayeh-Kumi, *The Ghanaian Times*, March 5, 1966.

10. Republic constitution, Article 18. A Presidential Commission of three was appointed by him—Nathaniel Welbeck being one of them—before his departure for Hanoi on February 21, 1966. The persons selected for this task, as for most others, were political nonentities, without following or standing in the country. No serious observer could ever have expected these Commissioners to be able to act in an emergency. The constitutional provisions concerning presidential succession were totally meaningless since there existed no body capable of selecting and agreeing on a successor. This included the Central Committee of the party and the cabinet.

11. Christian Bay, "Politics and Pseudopolitics . . .," *The American Political Science Review*, Vol. LIX, No. 1 (March, 1965).

12. See Lewis, *op. cit.*, pp. 62–63. Huntington, *op. cit.*, pp. 416–17, reminds us of the interest taken in the corrupt state by Plato, Aristotle, and Machiavelli.

13. Harvey, *op. cit.*, p. 238.

14. Cf. Simon Kuznets in Otto Feinstein (ed.), *Two Worlds of Change* (Garden City, N.Y.: Doubleday, 1964), pp. 1–21; also Karl de Schweinitz, Jr., "Economics and Underdeveloped Economies," *The American Behavioral Scientist*, IX, No. 1 (September, 1965), 5.

15. For a background and evaluation of the project, see Birmingham, Neustadt, and Omaboe (eds.), *op. cit.*, chap. xvi, "The Volta River Project"; see also "Nkrumah at the Volta," *West Africa*, January 22, 1966, p. 91. Ironically, Nkrumah's foreign and domestic policies, quarrels with Ghana's neighbors, and overextension at home, coupled with mismanagement of Ghana's finances, if allowed to continue, would have seriously endangered the economic potential of the project.

16. If taken at face value, the annual outlay for social services was remarkable, e.g., in 1963–64, 31 per cent of government expendi-

ture was spent for social services as against 29 per cent for economic services. In spite of the worsening economic conditions, Nkrumah persisted in earmarking percentages of similar magnitude for education and health services. However, the *real* gains for Ghana were considerably less than what would be suggested by these figures. The spreading corruption, mismanagement, and intellectual attrition, which were encouraged by the regime, took their toll as the allocations for social services outran available as well as potentially available economic resources, thus further weakening the country. See Birmingham, Neustadt, and Omaboe (eds.), *op. cit.*, pp. 28, 460–61. The Ghanaian case suggests caution in the application of purely quantitative development indices to sociopolitical analysis. According to such tests Ghana should perhaps have had a different political structure. See Everett E. Hagen, "A Framework for Analyzing Economic Change," in Robert E. Asher and others, *Development of the Emerging Countries* (Washington, D.C.: The Brookings Institution, 1962), p. 5.

17. *West Africa*, October 9, 1965, p. 1123; *Economic Survey, 1964*, p. 30.
18. Amoako-Atta, budget speech, quoted in *The Ghanaian Times*, February 22, 1966.
19. *West Africa*, October 23, 1965, p. 1193; *Rebirth of Ghana*, p. 38.
20. *Economic Survey, 1964* (Accra: Government Printer, pp. 30–31, 32. In order to keep up with the population growth rate of 2.6 per cent per annum, an economic growth rate of 5 per cent was considered necessary. (Birmingham, Neustadt, and Omaboe [eds.], *op. cit.*, p. 24.)
21. See "Commitments Arising out of Loans and Supplies Credit: Schedule Showing Commitments Entered into as at 30th November, 1964," *The Budget, 1965* (Accra: Ministry of Finance, 1965), Table IX, p. 41. The ambitious program must be read against comments that appeared in the budget's section, "The Financial Position of the State Corporations" (pp. 1 and 2):

> One of the main problems facing the enterprises is the lack of knowledgeable personnel. Often the "accountants," are not qualified, most of them having been mere bookkeepers with some experience. The Management of these corporations are themselves sometimes quite ignorant of development affecting their enterprises or ill-informed about them. . . . For purposes of this first exercise [by the Ministry of Finance] however, the present state of accounting staff of most of the enterprises is such that much reliance cannot be placed on their explanations of the balance sheet items. . . .

Of 32 enterprises included in that survey, only 3 reported profits. In terms of Government investment and Government loans applied to the 32 enterprises almost 30 per cent loss was incurred by 3 enterprises, one-third of the total loss credited to the prestigious Ghana Airways.

See also Birmingham, Neustadt, and Omaboe (eds.), *op. cit.*, pp. 30, 460–61. The total of fifty-two given in the text refers to the number of state-owned and mixed-ownership enterprises in operation in February, 1966.

22. Using his one-factor analysis, Nkrumah told the public that he would not allow the manipulators of the price of cocoa to hold up social development, school and hospital construction, etc. (*Debates*, August 24, 1965, col. 25.)

23. *West Africa*, April 24, 1965, p. 445; *Daily Graphic*, April 15, 1965; *The Ghanaian Times*, May 1, 1965.

24. *The Ghanaian Times*, April 19, 1965.

25. See Kweku Akwei's comments on the deletions from the Abraham Report, in the *Evening News*, March 25, 1966. For evidence of earlier tampering with Commission reports, see *Report of Commission of Enquiry into Alleged Irregularities and Malpractices in Connection with the Issue of Import Licenses* (Akainya Report) (Accra: Ministry of Information and Broadcasting, 1964); also *Evening News*, April 5, 1966, and *The Ghanaian Times*, April 6, 1966, dealing with Nkrumah's role in suppression of evidence; and *Daily Graphic*, April 13, 1966.

26. The Minister of Finance attributed the economic crisis to the drop in the world price of cocoa coupled with "determination of Government to persist in socialist transformation of the economy." (*The Spark*, October 29, 1965, pp. 4–5.)

27. Letter to the Editor, signed Thomas Hodgkin, *The Times* (London), March 5, 1966.

28. Instead of the Ghanaian public's being influenced by the crude and ineffective propaganda, Nkrumah himself may well have been the prime victim of what Robert K. Merton calls the self-fulfilling prophecy: A set of applied myths bring about certain reactions—e.g., the myth of the perpetual imperialist aggression leads to virulent anti-Western reactions and outbursts which in turn provoke reactions in Western capitals which in turn are interpreted as proof of the validity of the original assertion.

29. One of the most penetrating statements on the futility of articulation without systematic inquiry into the meaning of words and of perceptions is Martin Landau, "Due Process of Inquiry," *The American Behavioral Scientist*, IX, No. 2 (October, 1965), 4–10. For discussion of one of the most ludicrous exercises in Nkru-

maist communication and training, see *The Ghanaian Times,* June 18, 1965. The article deals with the three-week "ideological" orientation seminar at Winneba ordered by Nkrumah for the edification of his ministers. One of the textbooks used by the "students" was *Consciencism.* Aside from the fact that the program was singularly unsuited for the avowed purposes of the seminar, there was, at that time, suspicion that the seminar had been ordered to keep the cabinet members under surveillance while Nkrumah was attending the Commonwealth Conference.

30. A curious aspect of Nkrumah's perception of international diplomacy was his belief that the President of the United States, Lyndon Johnson in this case, could be persuaded to accept his word on any given matter—notwithstanding his deeds—by the mere dispatch of a personal note. In part, this notion stemmed from misinformation fed him by W. M. Q. Halm, one-time Ghanaian Ambassador to the United States. Halm had assured him that Johnson "had the votes" to bring Congress around to his position any time he wanted to and that he did not have to be concerned with public opinion, the press, and all that. (Based on interviews with Halm and a high-ranking U.S. diplomat.)

31. Tibor Szamueli, "The Prophet of the Utterly Absurd," *The Spectator* (London), March 11, 1966, p. 281.

32. Nkrumah, *Consciencism,* p. 78.

33. Karl W. Deutsch, in his *Nerves of Government,* p. 230, discusses what he calls potential sources of failure of a political regime. He cites the "injunction of humility," as one of the more crucial foundation stones of government. He writes: "In its extended sense, humility has perhaps implied the avoidance of overestimating not only the importance of oneself but also the importance of one's immediate environment. . . . Humility involves a profoundly skeptical attitude toward one's own ability to achieve it, or to maintain it for any length of time. Insufferable conceit has been noted in men who had convinced themselves that they were humble."

34. In the 1965 budget speech, Minister of Finance Amoako-Atta included the following reference: "At this juncture I wish to repeat Osagyefo's appeal to Ghanaians who have funds abroad to use these funds to purchase Ghana Government Bearer Bonds. For this reason, arrangements are being made by the Bank of Ghana to sell these Bonds abroad. As Osagyefo explained, these Bonds do not bear the names of the purchasers and cannot therefore constitute a source of embarrassment to those Ghanaians who buy them abroad." ("1965 Budget Statement," *The Budget, 1965,* p. 19.) See also Twum, *Debates,* August 26, 1965. cols. 69–70; Ayeh-Kumi, *Rebirth of Ghana,* pp. 44–45. There is

no evidence of purchase of these Bonds by or on behalf of Nkrumah to repatriate funds which he invested abroad. ("Back to the Dawn Broadcast," *West Africa*, September 18, 1965, p. 1039; see also Conor Cruise O'Brien, in *The Observer* (London), February 25, 1966.)

35. Commissioner Harlley, *Daily Graphic*, March 11, 1966.
36. J. N. K. Taylor, *The Evening News*, March 28, 1966; Edusei, *ibid.*; Ayeh-Kumi, *Daily Graphic*, March 22, 1966; Baidoe-Ansah, *The Evening News*, March 29, 1966; Halm, *ibid.*; Tachie-Menson, *The Ghanaian Times*, April 1, 1966. See also "Financial Statement," in *The Budget, 1965*, p. 6.
37. The Reverend C. K. Dovlo, *Debates*, August 30, 1965, col. 165. It was evident that the special presidential watchdog, the Leader of Government Business, either was not on the floor at that moment or he had once again allowed his attention to lapse. At any rate, this type of candor was exceedingly rare—perhaps unique—in the National Assembly.
38. *Bulletin of the International Commission of Jurists*, No. 24 (December, 1965), p. 26. On March 26, 1965, Nkrumah commuted the death sentences for five "traitors" to twenty years each. (*The Ghanaian Times*, March 27, 1965.) To extract these sentences from an unwilling court and prepare the ground for more—the five had been acquitted of the same charges in December, 1963 —Nkrumah amended the constitution, dismissed several judges, forced a partially secret retrial before a hand-picked jury and judge, and allowed alteration of evidence on which the five had been acquitted at the first trial.
39. Dr. Danquah's first wife, Mabel Dove, advised Nkrumah of Danquah's poor and declining health in a letter dated December 6, 1964. (*Evening News*, March 11, 1966, p. 3.)

EPILOGUE

1. *Sunday Telegraph* (London), January 30, 1966. One explanation offered for Nkrumah's departure at that point was that he wanted to be out of the country when the bad news contained in the 1966 budget message was broken; as it happened, the news was released the day after his departure. Nasser's comment, to an interviewer, is of special relevance: "You know, when he came here on the way to Peking, Nkrumah said he wanted to talk about Viet-Nam. I said no, please let us talk about Ghana— because we had many bad reports of the situation. But it was no use; he did not seem worried at all." (Erskine B. Childers, "Nasser's Front Door," *The Guardian* [London], April 27, 1966, p. 10.)

2. *Debates*, February 1, 1966, cols. 2–3.

3. Alexander, *op. cit.*, p. 77.

4. Erica Powell, Nkrumah's long-time private secretary, quoted in Alexander, *op. cit.*, p. 25. See also Thomas Hodgkin's letter to *The Times* (London), March 5, 1966; Major General Sir Edward Spears' reply, *The Times*, March 9, 1966; and Basil Davidson's letter, *The New Statesman*, March 11, 1966, p. 336. Major General Alexander may also aid in the creation of a legend. Although his book offers ample evidence to the contrary, he asserts that Nkrumah found it hard to say no to anyone (p. 25). Nkrumah said no to virtually all of the able civil servants, to all counselors of economic reform and sound financial practice, to advocates of better relations with the West, and, obviously, he said no to Alexander a good deal of the time. Cf. testimony of the former Minister of Finance relating how Nkrumah dismissed bank directors who told him about the state of chaos in the financial structure. (*The Ghanaian Times*, March 25, 1966.)

5. John Davies, Jr., quoted in Schlesinger, *op. cit.*, p. 198.

6. *Ibid.*, p. 205.

Selected Bibliography

BOOKS

ALEXANDER, MAJOR GENERAL H. T. *African Tightrope: My Two Years as Nkrumah's Chief of Staff*. London: Pall Mall Press, 1965; New York: Frederick A. Praeger, 1966.

APTER, DAVID. *Ghana in Transition*. New York: Atheneum, 1963.

————. *The Gold Coast in Transition*. Princeton, N.J.: Princeton University Press, 1955.

ARMAH, KWESI. *Africa's Golden Road*. London: Heinemann, 1965.

AUSTIN, DENNIS. *Politics in Ghana, 1946–1960*. London and New York: Oxford University Press, 1964.

BIRMINGHAM, W. B.; NEUSTADT, I.; and OMABOE, E. N. (eds.). *A Study of Contemporary Ghana*. Vol. I: *The Economy of Ghana*. London: Allen & Unwin, 1966.

BOURRET, F. M. *Ghana: The Road to Independence, 1919–1957*. Stanford, Calif.: Stanford University Press; London: Oxford University Press, 1960.

BRETTON, HENRY L. *Power and Stability in Nigeria: The Politics of Decolonization*. New York: Frederick A. Praeger; London: Pall Mall Press, 1962.

BROCKWAY, FENNER. *African Socialism*. London: The Bodley Head, 1963.

COLEMAN, JAMES S., and ROSBERG, CARL G., JR. (eds.). *Political Parties and National Integration in Tropical Africa*. Berkeley, Calif.: University of California Press, 1964.

DEI-ANANG, MICHAEL. *Ghana Resurgent*. Accra: Waterville Publishing House, 1964.

DEUTSCH, KARL W. *The Nerves of Government: Models of Political Communication and Control*. New York: The Free Press of Glencoe, 1963.

DEUTSCH, KARL W., and FOLITZ, WILLIAM J. (eds.). *Nation-Building*. New York: Atherton Press, 1963.

DZIRASA, THE REVEREND STEPHEN. *Political Thought of Kwame Nkrumah*. Accra: Guinea Press, n.d., [probably 1961 or 1962].

FRIEDLAND, W. H., and ROSBERG, JR., CARL G. (eds.). *African Socialism*. Stanford, Calif.: Stanford University Press, 1964.

HANNA, WILLIAM J. *Independent Black Africa*. Chicago: Rand McNally, 1964.

HARVEY, WILLIAM B. *Law and Social Change in Ghana*. Princeton, N.J.: Princeton University Press, 1966.

HUXLEY, ELSPETH. *Four Guineas*. London: Chatto & Windus, 1954.

219

ITALIAANDER, ROLF. *The New Leaders of Africa.* London: Prentice-Hall International, 1961.

LEWIS, W. ARTHUR. *Politics in West Africa.* London: Allen & Unwin, 1965.

METCALFE, G. E. *Great Britain and Ghana: Documents of Ghana History, 1807–1957.* London and Legon: Thomas Nelson for the University of Ghana, 1964.

NKRUMAH, KWAME. *Africa Must Unite.* New York: Frederick A. Praeger; London: Heinemann, 1963.

—— *Consciencism.* London: Heinemann, 1964; New York: Monthly Review Press, 1965.

—— *Ghana: The Autobiography of Kwame Nkrumah.* London and New York: Thomas Nelson, 1957.

—— *I Speak of Freedom: A Statement of African Ideology.* London: Heinemann; New York: Frederick A. Praeger, 1961.

—— *Neo-Colonialism: The Last Stage of Imperialism.* London: Thomas Nelson, 1965.

—— *Towards Colonial Freedom.* London: Heinemann, 1962.

PADMORE, GEORGE. *The Gold Coast Revolution.* London: Dennis Dobson, 1953.

PHILLIPS, JOHN. *Kwame Nkrumah and The Future of Africa.* London: Faber & Faber; New York: Frederick A. Praeger, 1960.

POWELL, ERICA. *Kwame Nkrumah of the New Africa.* London: Thomas Nelson, 1965.

QUAISON-SACKEY, ALEX. *Africa Unbound: Reflections of an African Statesman.* New York: Frederick A. Praeger; London: Andre Deutsch, 1963.

RUBIN, L., and MURRAY, P. *The Constitution and Government of Ghana.* London: Sweet & Maxwell, 1961.

The Spark, *Some Essential Features of Nkrumaism.* London: Lawrence & Wishart, 1964.

OFFICIAL PUBLICATIONS

Acts of Ghana. Accra, Government Printer.

The Annual Estimates for 1963–64. Part I: *Consolidated Fund.* Vols. I–XVI. Accra: Government Printer, 1964.

The Annual Estimates for 1965. Part I: *Consolidated Fund.* Vol. I: *The President,* Vol. V: *Defence,* Vol. IX: *Foreign Affairs,* Vol. XIII: *Interior.* Vol. XVI: *Extra Ministerial.* Accra: Government Printer, 1965.

Annual Report on the Treatment of Offenders for the Calendar Year 1962. Accra: Ministry of Information and Broadcasting, 1965.

The Budget, 1965. Accra: The Ministry of Finance, 1965.

Commission of Enquiry into Mr. Braimah's Resignation and Allega-

tions Arising Therefrom. (Korsah Commission.) Accra: Government Printer, 1954.

Economic Survey 1963. Accra: Ministry of Information and Broadcasting, 1964.

Economic Survey 1964. Accra: Ministry of Information and Broadcasting, 1965.

First Report from the Public Accounts Committee of the National Assembly, and *Second Report from the Public Accounts Committee of the National Assembly.* Accra, 1964.

Ghana Gazette. Accra, Government Printer.

Government Organisation Manual. Vol. I. Accra: Organisation and Methods Secretariat, 1965.

Handbook on State Corporations. Accra: State Enterprises Secretariat, 1965.

Parliamentary Debates, Official Record (cited as *Debates*). Accra, Government Printer.

The Rebirth of Ghana. Accra: The Ministry of Information for the National Liberation Council, 1966.

Report of Commission of Enquiry into Alleged Irregularities and Malpractices in Connection with the Issue of Import Licenses. Accra: Ministry of Information and Broadcasting, 1964.

Report of the Commission of Enquiry into Disturbances in the Gold Coast, 1948. (The Watson Report.) London: HMSO, 1948.

Report of the Commission of Enquiry into Trade Malpractices in Ghana. (The Abraham Report.) Accra: Office of the President, 1966.

Revised Report of the Delimitation Commission, 1964. Accra: Office of the President, 1965.

Seven-Year Development Plan: Annual Plan for the Second Plan Year, 1965 Financial Year. Ministry of Information and Broadcasting, 1965.

Towards the Referendum. Accra: Ministry of Information and Broadcasting, 1964.

ARTICLES

ANDRAIN, CHARLES F. "Patterns of African Socialist Thought," *African Forum,* I, No. 3 (Winter, 1966), 48–49.

BRETTON, HENRY L. "Current Political Thought and Practice in Ghana," *The American Political Science Review,* LII, No. 1 (March, 1958), 46–63.

GREEN, REGINALD. "Four African Development Plans," *The Journal of Modern African Studies,* III, No. 2 (1965), 249–79.

HUNTINGTON, SAMUEL P. "Political Development and Political Decay," *World Politics,* XVII, No. 3 (April, 1965), 386–430.

PERIODICALS AND NEWSPAPERS

The Spark (Accra). 1964–66.
The Ghanaian Times (Accra). 1964-66.
Evening News (Accra). 1964–66.
Daily Graphic (Accra). 1964–66.
West Africa (Accra). 1956–66.

Index

223

A